T0013924

HOMEMADE ROBOTS

HOMEMADE ROBOTS

10 Simple Bots to Build with Stuff Around the House

BY RANDY SARAFAN

**no starch
press**

San Francisco

Homemade Robots. Copyright © 2021 by Randy Sarafan.

All rights reserved. No part of this work may be reproduced or transmitted in any form or by any means, electronic or mechanical, including photocopying, recording, or by any information storage or retrieval system, without the prior written permission of the copyright owner and the publisher.

Printed in Korea

First printing

25 24 23 22 21   1 2 3 4 5 6 7 8 9

ISBN-13: 978-1-7185-0023-5 (print)
ISBN-13: 978-1-7185-0024-2 (ebook)

Publisher: William Pollock
Executive Editor: Barbara Yien
Production Manager: Rachel Monaghan
Production Editor: Dapinder Dosanjh
Developmental Editors: Jill Franklin and Patrick DiJusto
Cover Illustrator: Monica Kamsvaag
Interior Design: Maureen Forys, Happenstance Type-O-Rama
Technical Reviewer: Becky Stern
Copyeditor: Bart Reed
Compositor: Maureen Forys, Happenstance Type-O-Rama
Proofreader: Lisa Devoto Farrell

For information on book distributors or translations, please contact No Starch Press, Inc. directly:
No Starch Press, Inc.
245 8th Street, San Francisco, CA 94103
phone: 1-415-863-9900; info@nostarch.com
www.nostarch.com

Library of Congress Cataloging-in-Publication Data
Names: Sarafan, Randy, author.
Title: Homemade robots : 10 simple bots to build with stuff around the house
    / Randy Sarafan.
Description: San Francisco : No Starch Press, 2021. | Includes
    bibliographical references and index.
Identifiers: LCCN 2021010148 (print) | LCCN 2021010149 (ebook) | ISBN
    9781718500235 (print) | ISBN 9781718500242 (ebook)
Subjects: LCSH: Robots--Design and construction--Amateurs' manuals.
Classification: LCC TJ211.15 .S27 2021 (print) | LCC TJ211.15 (ebook) |
    DDC 629.8/92--dc23
LC record available at https://lccn.loc.gov/2021010148
LC ebook record available at https://lccn.loc.gov/2021010149

No Starch Press and the No Starch Press logo are registered trademarks of No Starch Press, Inc. Other product and company names mentioned herein may be the trademarks of their respective owners. Rather than use a trademark symbol with every occurrence of a trademarked name, we are using the names only in an editorial fashion and to the benefit of the trademark owner, with no intention of infringement of the trademark.

The information in this book is distributed on an "As Is" basis, without warranty. While every precaution has been taken in the preparation of this work, neither the author nor No Starch Press, Inc. shall have any liability to any person or entity with respect to any loss or damage caused or alleged to be caused directly or indirectly by the information contained in it.

*This book is dedicated
to anyone who ever wanted to
build a robot but was too scared to try.*

About the Author

Randy Sarafan creates interactive objects that inject fun and whimsy into everyday life. His previous book, *62 Projects to Make with a Dead Computer*, makes computer reuse fun and accessible. Randy's work has been celebrated in books, newspapers, magazines, tabloids, academic journals, news blogs, and on television, radio, and podcasts. For more than a decade, Randy has worked for Instructables (Autodesk) where he created hundreds of DIY project tutorials on everything from making pancakes to building giant rideable robots. He received an MFA from San Francisco State University in Digital Media and Emerging Technology and a BFA from Parsons School of Design in Design and Technology. Visit his website at *http://randysarafan.com/* to see all of his new and exciting projects.

About the Technical Reviewer

Becky Stern has authored hundreds of DIY tutorials about everything from microcontrollers to knitting. She is currently a product manager at Instructables (Autodesk). Before joining Instructables, Becky worked as a senior video producer for *Make:* magazine and as director of wearable electronics at Adafruit. She lives in New York City and enjoys riding on two wheels, making YouTube videos, and collecting new hobbies to share with others.

BRIEF CONTENTS

CONTENTS IN DETAIL

ACKNOWLEDGMENTS

I first want to thank Bill Pollock at No Starch Press for taking a chance on this slightly unusual book and letting me stay true to my artistic vision.

I'd also like to thank all of the wonderful and hardworking folks at No Starch Press who helped create something of which we can all be proud: Barbara Yien, Dapinder Dosanjh, Jill Franklin, Patrick DiJusto, Bart Reed, Becky Stern, and everyone else who worked to make this book happen.

Another big thank you goes out to Eric Wilhelm. Without his initial support, this book may have never come about.

I'd also like to thank my community of peers who never cease to amaze and inspire me.

Finally, I would like to thank my utterly amazing wife, Jenn. Her endless patience and encouragement helped me see this book through to the end.

INTRODUCTION

The idea of building robots can seem daunting, but you don't need to be an engineer, scientist, or wizard to get started. You need only some basic know-how and an open mind. Throughout this book, I'll provide the knowledge you need to begin building robots. In exchange, I'm counting on you to be creative, inquisitive, and determined.

Robots come in many different types. Some robots, called *humanoids*, are smart and humanlike. These are the kinds you typically see in movies and are probably most familiar with. Other robots are more abstract and sculptural. *BEAM robots*, for example, are small sculptural robots built on the principle of Biology, Electronics, Aesthetics, and Mechanisms. These robots perform simple actions using basic recycled electronic components. Between those two extremes is an entire universe of different types of robots—too many to name here.

The robots you'll be making in this book are closer in spirit to BEAM robots. In fact, I like to call them "bots" because, like the word *bot*, these robots themselves are a bit abbreviated, so you can think of the bots described here as bare-bones starting points for future robotic exploration.

All of the bots in this book adhere to the same basic set of rules:

- They are quick and easy to build with readily available materials.
- They are easy to understand and don't require a microcontroller or computer programming.
- They are mobile and autonomous (that is, self-driving).
- They are expandable, allowing you to incorporate more complex electronic controls later.

Are Bots Alive?

No, but they pretend to be. Hold on to your hats as I delve into some theory.

Think about this: fallen leaves blowing in the wind are almost perfectly random, and pistons moving in an engine are almost perfectly mechanical. An object begins taking on living attributes when it has *predictable unpredictability*—that is, not totally random and not totally mechanized. To understand how this works, let's take a detour into the world of video games.

A gaming concept called a *core mechanic* is a behavior that a player performs over and over again during gameplay. An example of this is continuously pressing the "fire" button on a controller. Another is making a character jump from platform to platform repeatedly.

With each bot you'll build, the core mechanic is the essence of its main behavior. It could be driving forward or backward, spinning in circles, rolling, or jumping. Each bot will have one predictable behavior that seems to come before all the others.

Yet, as I've mentioned, predictability alone does not make an object seem alive. Something that simply spins in circles isn't very lifelike. What gives bots the illusion of being alive? Unpredictable behavior. A bot's personality comes from occasional deviations from its core mechanic. For instance, if a bot drives in circles, it's easy to think of it as a machine, but if that same bot tips over and then rights itself, you find yourself thinking it's clumsy. In this way, it transforms from being a machine that performs a repetitive task to one that has personality.

Some thought experiments may help you understand this concept. What would make a flock of birds seem robotic? What would it take to make an elevator seem like a living organism?

How Should Bots Behave?

If the goal is to make a robot seem alive, what creature should it behave like? Some people like to make bots that act like humans or other living beings. This is a mistake. Bots should be allowed to be themselves and behave however they want. If a bot spins in place three times and then jumps forward, it should be allowed to move like that even though it's not a natural movement for an animal. In other words, bots should imitate the *idea* of living things. They don't have to be a substitute for any existing lifeform.

Put another way, a bot should not act like a zebra any more than a zebra should act like a bot. The bot should behave like it's alive without mirroring any particular lifeform. A bot can be inspired or informed by living creatures, but it should not seek to replicate any directly. Why try to repeat something that already does what it does? It's a disservice to the robot race to force bots to try to repeat "actual" living behaviors. Bots should develop their own. After all, what makes bots interesting is their ability to develop behaviors that organic creatures do not and often cannot.

In Summary

A successful bot is a mechanical device that is quickly and easily built and understood. It's mobile and autonomous, and it has potential for evolution. It has predictable behavior that occasionally changes unpredictably, and it should be allowed to be itself (and not a zebra).

Obviously, this definition alone doesn't actually teach you how to build a bot. Fret not; you're getting there. But first, let's review all the tools and techniques you'll need to get started.

> **NOTE** This book presents just one approach to building robots that I've found to be not only compelling, but also a highly effective starting point. Try building these bots and learn my method, but also be sure to explore different approaches and ideas. A wide world of robots is yours to discover.

1

BUILDING TOOLS AND SUPPLIES

To make some basic robots, you first need some tools. Almost all the tools you'll use in the creation of your friendly little bots are basic hand tools. In fact, you'll be using only a very limited number of power tools, but more on that in a bit.

You probably already have most of the tools you'll need lying around the house, and I am going to assume you already understand the basic operating principle of something like a hammer or screwdriver.

For those of you who have never used a power drill before, I'll go over it briefly. If you've already got that down, skim through this section and perhaps discover some new and useful tips, or feel free to skip ahead to the sections on fasteners and materials.

Your toolbox should contain the following tools:

Tools

- ➡ Power drill and drill bits
- ➡ A hammer
- ➡ Screwdrivers (Phillips and slotted)
- ➡ Pliers
- ➡ Cutting pliers
- ➡ Wire stripper

- ➡ Scissors
- ➡ A box cutter
- ➡ A hacksaw
- ➡ C-clamps
- ➡ A bench vise

Drills and Drill Bits

The primary power tool you'll be using in this book is a power drill. It does not matter whether yours is battery powered or corded; however, I prefer to use a corded drill because it's cheaper and won't run out of power while I'm working.

In addition to the drill, you'll need some general-purpose *split point drill bits*. These are what the drill spins to cut holes in objects. The drill will always make a hole that's the same width as the drill bit you are using, so try to find a drill bit set that includes a variety of sizes. Buying a set is an easy and economical way to make sure you are able to drill a wide variety of holes. Sets that you find at the hardware store typically range in size from ¹⁄₁₆ inch up to ½ inch in diameter.

You'll also be using *spade bits* in this book. This type of drill bit consists of a center point and outside cutting edges called *spurs*. The *center point* makes a small hole in the middle of what you are drilling. This keeps the spade in place as the spurs cut a much larger outer hole. This type of drill bit is used to cut holes wider than ½ inch. The spade bit size you'll use most is ¾ inch.

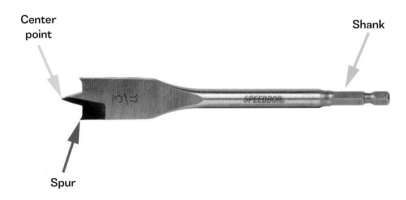

Center point

Shank

Spur

To get started, locate the rotating assembly at the front of the drill where you insert the drill bit. This is called the *chuck*, and it has jaws inside that open and close to grab onto the drill bit.

To open the jaws of the chuck, twist it counterclockwise until the jaws are slightly wider than the drill bit. Insert a drill bit into the chuck so there's some space between the end of the chuck and the drill bit's spiral cutting flutes. Twist the chuck clockwise until its jaws clamp down on the shank of the drill bit.

When the drill is in use, the drill bit should not wobble while spinning. In other words, the drill bit should spin entirely on-center. If it appears to be mounted off-center, remove the drill bit and go through the process of inserting it again.

Wrong   Right

Nearly all modern drills allow you to control the drill bit's speed and rotation direction. You usually change rotation direction (clockwise or counterclockwise) with a switch found near the drill's trigger button, and how hard you press the trigger button determines the speed. The harder you press, the faster the drill bit spins.

Direction   Speed

Before using any drill, first clamp down the object you want to drill with your bench vise or C-clamps.

Place the point of the drill bit perpendicular to the surface you want to drill through, and slowly bring the drill bit up to speed. Gently press down on the drill until you are all the way through the surface.

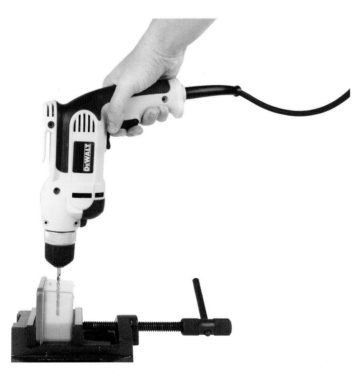

Fasteners and Adhesives

Once you've drilled a bunch of holes through objects, you can attach them together with fasteners. You'll mainly encounter two types of mechanical fasteners when building robots: *zip ties* and *nuts and bolts*.

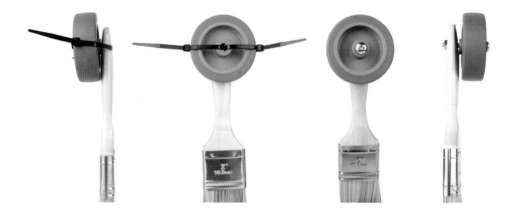

You'll use zip ties in basically every project in this book. Zip ties are easy to use to attach things together, and they're easy to undo if you make a mistake. They're strong, they don't easily break or snap, and they're also cheap and readily available—all great attributes for building simple robots.

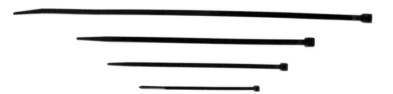

To use a zip tie, simply stick the "tail" end into the little "mouth" end and pull it tight. You'll hear the plastic make a "zip" noise as it's pulled through. Notice how once it has been tightened, it cannot be loosened. This is both a benefit and a curse. If you mess up, the only way to undo the zip tie is with cutting pliers or scissors.

In addition to zip ties, some robots may use nuts and bolts, which are also easy to use and come in a variety of sizes. Nuts and bolts have two standards of measurement: imperial and metric. In the US, the standard is imperial, so everything is measured in inches and fractions of an inch. Metric is used in the rest of the world. This book is primarily written for a US audience, so I'll use imperial measurements.

Nuts and bolts have two measurements that describe them. The first is the width of the bolt, and the second is the thread spacing. For instance, a ¼-20 bolt is ¼ inch wide and has 20 threads per inch. A ½-13 bolt is ½ inch wide and has 13 threads per inch.

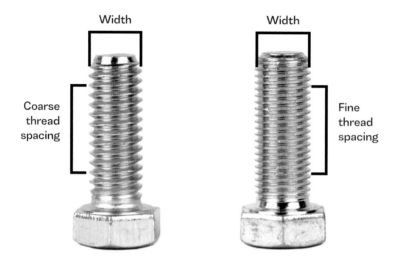

Nuts and bolts will thread together *only* if the width and thread count match.

To use a nut and bolt, insert the bolt through both holes in the two objects you want to attach together. Once the bolt is passed through both objects, twist the nut clockwise to fasten the objects together.

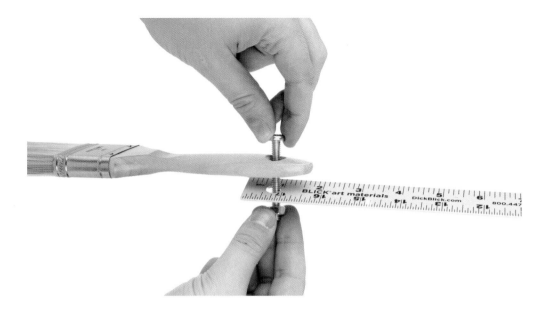

On occasion in this book, or in your own exploration, you'll need some other specialized fastening hardware, which you should be able to find in your local hardware store. However, you might need to order something online. See the "Basic Electronics Shopping List" in Appendix A for resources.

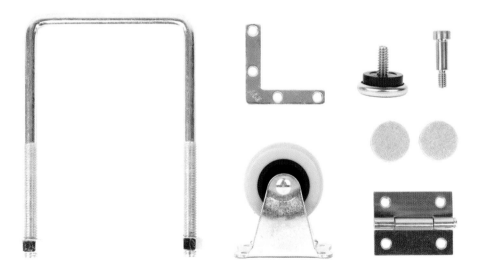

The other way to attach objects together is with an adhesive, most commonly with glue or tape. It is always preferable to use mechanical fasteners over adhesives since they're easier to undo. That said, on a few occasions in this book you'll attach things with adhesives—primarily when you use painter's tape to temporarily attach paper drill templates to objects. One project (the Skitter Bot) uses glue, which I'll cover in Chapter 10.

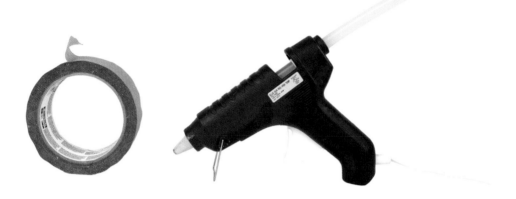

Alternative Materials

This book doesn't require any fixed set of materials or a building kit. You can build these bots using stuff you find around the house, and you may not find the exact parts used here. I'll describe the parts as best I can in the materials list for each bot, but you can improvise with what is available to you. For instance, if the book calls for using a plastic container as the robot body, you could potentially swap it out with a cardboard or wooden box. Also, you might replace a wheel made from a CD with a large, round bike reflector. The idea is that you observe the basic shapes and materials for the different components and simply replace them with what you have on hand. Aside from the electronics, rarely is a part so specific that it cannot be swapped out.

To the frustration of many serious engineers, I often like to say, "building bots isn't an exact science." However, this is only a half-truth. A great deal of robotics uses precise scientific principles, but this book explores the part of robotics that requires creativity, ingenuity, and experimentation. It's intended to inspire you to play, improvise, and innovate. Think of the directions as guidelines, and feel free to change them to suit your purposes.

Once you get good at building bots, if you really want to go wild, you can even swap out the parts with unusual building materials, such as old stuffed animals or even food.

2

GETTING STARTED WITH ELECTRONICS

One of the most daunting aspects of learning robotics is getting a grasp on the electronics. Although the subject matter is vast and can be highly technical, with some basic information, almost anyone can get electricity to work for them. Luckily for you, I am here to provide that information. All that is required is patience and a willingness to learn. Some of this information might not make sense right away, and that is okay. As you actually begin to build some bots, everything will start to become clear.

Batteries and Electricity

In this book, all of the electricity used will come from batteries. When you're using a battery, remember that electrical current always flows between a voltage source and ground. You've likely noticed that batteries have a plus (positive) side and a minus (negative) side. By tradition, the minus side of the battery is the ground, and the plus side is the positive voltage.

Ground   Voltage

An electric charge can have two attributes: *current* (the amount of electric charge in a circuit) and *voltage* (the force by which the charge is flowing through the circuit). If you think of a circuit like a garden hose, the current is how much water is flowing through it, and the voltage is the force by which the water is being pushed through.

Typical cylindrical batteries, from AAA all the way up to D batteries, can provide 1.5 V of electricity. The difference between these batteries is not how much voltage they can provide but how much current they can provide. The larger the battery, the more current it can provide and the longer it will provide electricity.

Circuits

Now that you understand more about batteries, you may be wondering how to use them to power a circuit that uses a voltage higher than 1.5 V. The answer is simple: you connect the batteries *in series* to achieve higher voltages. This means placing the batteries end to end, where the positive side of one touches the ground side of the next. The voltage of all the batteries in the series is added together, so by connecting four 1.5 V batteries end to end, you can easily create a 6 V power source.

A *battery holder* is an enclosure designed to connect batteries in series. The more batteries in a battery holder, the higher the voltage. You can calculate the total voltage of a battery holder by multiplying the number of the batteries by 1.5.

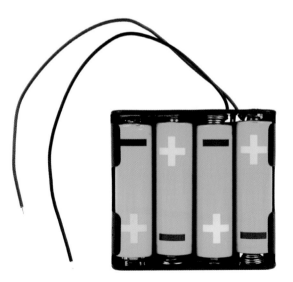

1.5 V × 4 batteries = 6 V

WIRES

You can see that the battery pack has a red wire and a black wire coming out of it. In *DC (direct current)* electronics, the red wire from a battery pack is always the power connection, and the black wire is always the ground.

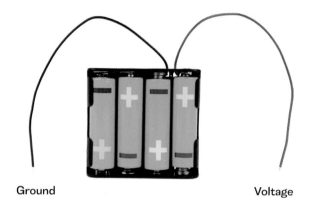

Ground   Voltage

To connect a battery pack to anything else, you need a conductive wire. A *conductor* is material that easily lets electricity flow. For all the robot projects, you'll be using insulated wire. An *insulator* is material that prevents the flow of electricity across it. By using an insulated wire with a conductive core, you can route electricity to the places it needs to go, without worrying about the wires touching and making incorrect connections.

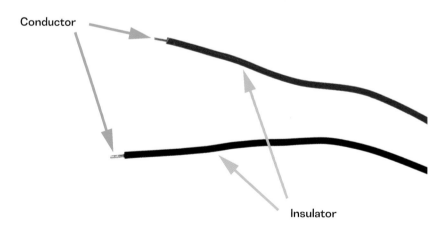

Conductor

Insulator

In order to use insulated wire, you need to strip off some insulation from the end of the wire. I find it's best to strip off from ½ inch to 1 inch of insulation. Anything less may be challenging to work with, and anything more may expose too much wire and result in crossed connections.

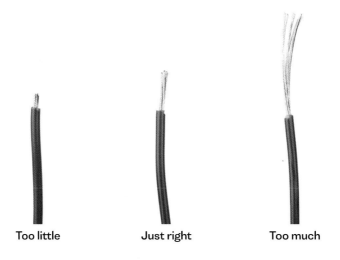

Too little   Just right   Too much

TEST LEADS WITH ALLIGATOR CLIPS

Test leads with *alligator clips* are great for temporarily making electrical connections between different electrical wires. To use them, press down on the back of the alligator clip, place whatever you are trying to grab onto its jaws, and release to clamp down.

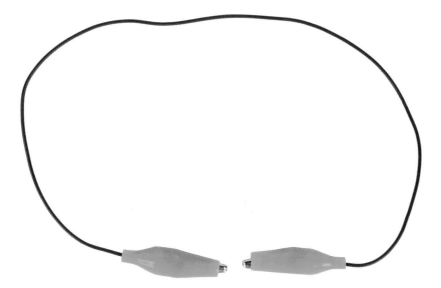

Alligator clips will be effective only if they are chomping down on a conductor.

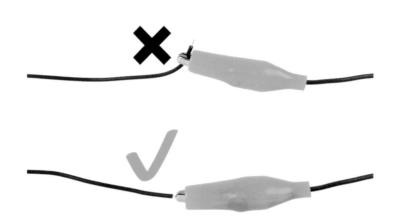

You can use test leads to connect a battery pack to different electronic components. If the components are connected in a way that allows electricity to flow between the power source and ground, you have created a circuit. A *circuit* is simply a complete path between power and ground.

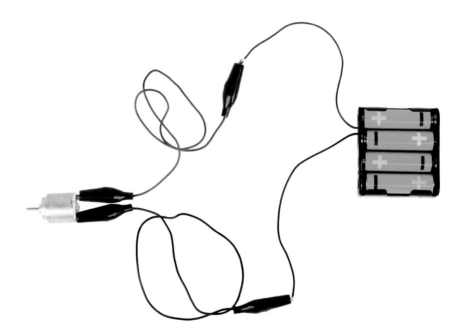

SHORT CIRCUITS

If you decide you want to bypass all of the electronics and create the simplest of circuits by connecting two battery pack wires together (don't), congratulations, you have just created a short circuit!

A *short circuit* is a circuit that does not have a load between the positive side of the circuit and the ground side of the circuit to use the energy. A *load* is basically anything that uses electrical energy.

> ⚡ **WARNING** Do not ever intentionally create a short circuit!

When a battery's positive voltage terminal is directly connected to the ground terminal, there is nothing to "use up" the energy that flows down the wire. With the electrons flowing only a short distance, they build up large amounts of heat. This causes the electronic components themselves to begin to heat up, melt, and possibly catch on fire, which is obviously a bad state of affairs. Check out this wire that melted during a short circuit:

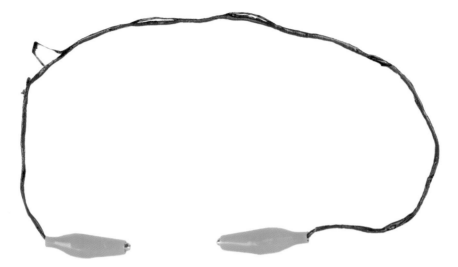

A very alarming hint that you have created a short circuit is seeing "magic smoke," which appears suddenly and seems to flow mysteriously from inside your electric circuit. If you see this smoke, quickly disconnect the power.

It is important to always connect a power supply to a load. For the purposes of this book, the easiest thing to connect a power supply to is a motor. Motors use lots of energy.

SWITCHES

To control the flow of power in a circuit, you'll need a *switch*, which is a mechanical device that alternately breaks or completes an electrical circuit. A switch is literally two pieces of metal that are either touching each other (closed) or broken apart (open).

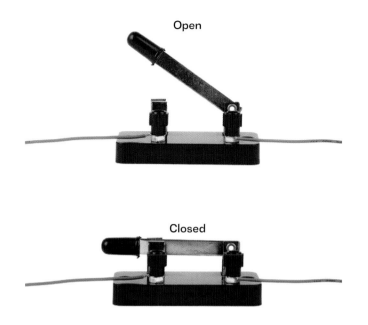

Open

Closed

The most basic type of switch opens and closes one mechanical connection and controls one electrical circuit. This is called a *single-pole single-throw (SPST)* switch. The *pole* is the point where an electrical current enters the circuit, and the *throw* is a potential output point.

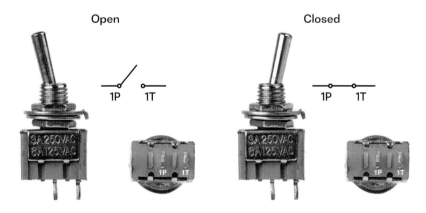

Open

Closed

1P 1T

1P 1T

Switches with a single throw are easy to use because they have only one output, but a switch with more than one throw can have different outputs, depending on how it is toggled. For instance, a *single-pole double-throw (SPDT)* switch has a single pole to which a common connection is attached, but it has a double throw that allows it to toggle between two different output connections. When switched one way, it outputs toward its *normally closed (NC)* connection, and when toggled the opposite way, it routes electricity through its *normally open (NO)* connection.

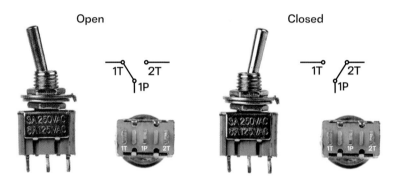

Some switches can even have more than one pole, such as the *double-pole double-throw (DPDT)* switch shown next. This switch is like having two separate SPDT switches combined together in one switch. Each pole is a separate electrical input connection, and each one toggles through two separate electrical outputs.

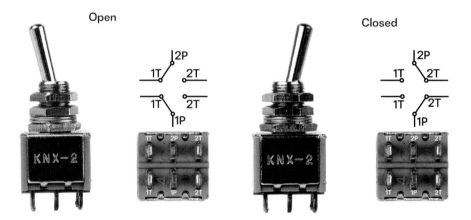

OTHER SWITCHES

Thus far I've been describing toggle switches, which are activated when pushed back and forth. However, many types of switches exist that are triggered in many different ways. In this book, you'll use a few different types of switches, including lever switches, reed (magnet) switches, and tilt switches.

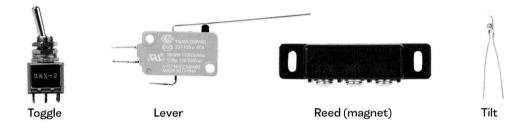

Toggle   Lever   Reed (magnet)   Tilt

Switches are typically activated by some sort of physical input. However, a *relay* is a type of switch that is activated by an electromagnet. When the coil of an electromagnet is powered up, the switch inside the relay is engaged, and when power is released, the switch inside the relay goes back to its normal state. In Chapters 13 and 14, you'll use relays to make some advanced circuits.

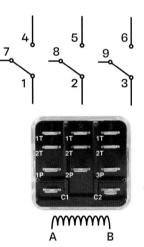

SERIES CIRCUITS

As you learned earlier in the chapter, to have something in series means to connect it in a line, one after another. In this case, the power wire from the battery pack goes through the switch, then through the motor, and finally to ground.

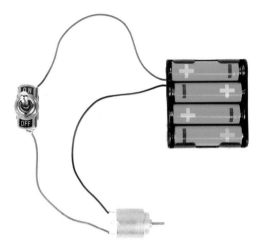

The power flows through each component in a series. If you were to break any of the connections in the circuit, as shown next, the power would turn off.

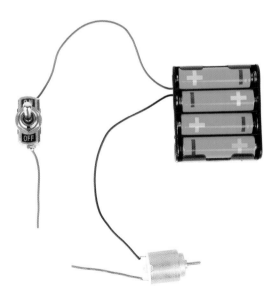

In the following circuit, the switch essentially serves the same function as disconnecting the wire. If the switch is toggled on, the connection is made and electricity is able to flow. If the switch is toggled off, the connection is disconnected, the series is broken, and no electricity can flow.

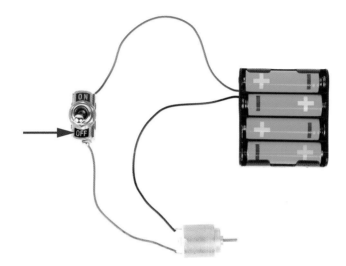

You can even wire two motors in series. However, you typically wouldn't do this, because when voltage has to pass through two coils in series to get to ground, you end up reducing the speed of both motors by about half. Or, to put it another way, twice as much voltage is required to power two motors at normal speed if they're connected in series.

PARALLEL CIRCUITS

It is better to wire the motors *in parallel*. In a parallel circuit, the loads are wired side by side with electricity passing through both at once in order to get to ground. In this arrangement, they both spin at normal speed at their normal voltage, but they now are drawing double the amount of current from the batteries. This configuration is better because a battery pack can typically provide more current, but it can't provide more voltage.

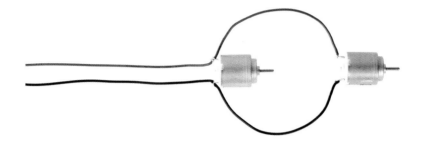

The other benefit of wiring motors in parallel is that even if you disconnect one motor from the power source, the other motor continues to be powered without disruption. So, if one motor fails or stalls, the other will keep working.

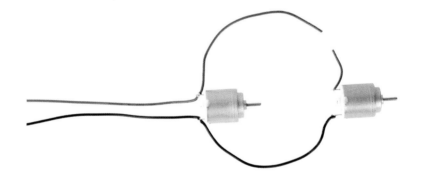

As a general rule for this book, motors should be wired only in parallel. In fact, all the bots you'll build that use two or more motors are wired in parallel. Sometimes they have a switch wired in series to one or both of the parallel motors. This allows the switches to turn on or off one or both motors. You'll learn more about motors in the next chapter.

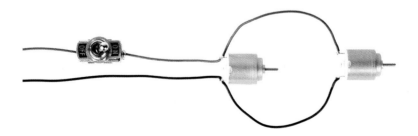

3

MOTORS

A robot's muscles are almost always its motors. Put simply, a *motor* is an electromechanical device that rotates a shaft when an electric current is applied to it. There are many kinds of motors, but the particular type of motor normally used for robotics is a DC (direct current) motor.

DC Motors

The most fundamental thing you need to understand about DC motors is that electromagnetic forces cause DC motors to spin. When power is applied to the motor's terminals, the motor shaft spins in one direction.

When you reverse the power wires to the terminals, the motor shaft spins in the opposite direction. This is because when you reverse the power to an electromagnet, the magnetic fields created inside the motor are also reversed.

H-Bridges

If you want to change the direction a motor is spinning using a switch, you need to create a circuit called an *H-bridge*, which is simply a circuit that allows a motor's direction to be reversed.

H-bridge

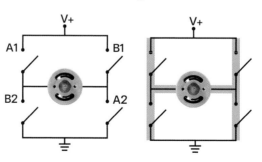

A basic H-bridge consists of two pairs of single-pole single-throw (SPST) switches. One pair is located between each motor terminal and the voltage source, and one pair is located between each motor terminal and ground. When you draw this out on paper, you'll notice it looks a bit like an *H*, which is how this circuit got its name.

When the set of switches labeled "A" is closed, power flows through the motor in such a way that it spins clockwise. When the other set, labeled "B," is closed, power flows in the opposite direction, and the motor spins counterclockwise.

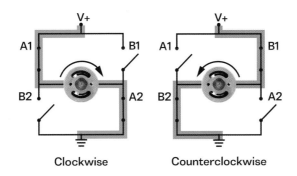

Clockwise   Counterclockwise

Both sets of switches cannot be closed at the same time. If you do this, power will be connected directly to ground, and you'll have just created the dreaded short circuit discussed in the previous chapter.

In addition, if you mix and match the switches, such as by closing A1 and B2, you'll also create a short circuit. It is important that only the "A" switches get closed or, alternatively, the "B" switches. There should never be some combination of the two.

Obviously, having to toggle four different switches is impractical and can lead to mistakes. Fortunately, you can replace all four SPST switches in the circuit with a single double-pole double-throw (DPDT) switch. With a DPDT switch, you can create the most basic H-bridge circuit imaginable.

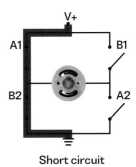

Short circuit

When the DPDT switch is toggled one way, the motor will spin clockwise, and when it is toggled the opposite way, the motor will reverse and spin counterclockwise.

To build your first H-bridge switch, solder the red wire from a 3 × AA battery holder to one of the center pins on your DPDT switch and the black wire to the other center pin (see Chapter 4 for detailed soldering instructions).

Next, select one of the pairs of outer pins. Solder a red motor wire to the switch terminal in line with the center pin that has the red battery holder wire attached. Then solder a black motor wire to the other outer pin.

Now when the switch is toggled, the motor is either powered by the battery pack and spinning clockwise or doing nothing at all.

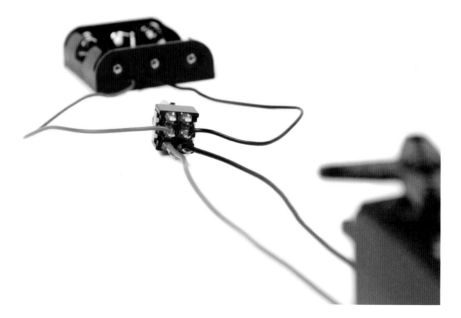

That's a positive first step, but remember, you actually want the motor to change direction when the switch is toggled, not turn off. To make this happen, you need to figure out a way to reverse the power to the motor.

REVERSING POWER TO THE MOTOR

To make the H-bridge fully functional, you need to wire the switch's remaining pins in such a way as to reverse the power to the motor. All you need to do is make a crisscrossed wire connection from the unused outer pair of switch terminals to the terminals connected to the motor.

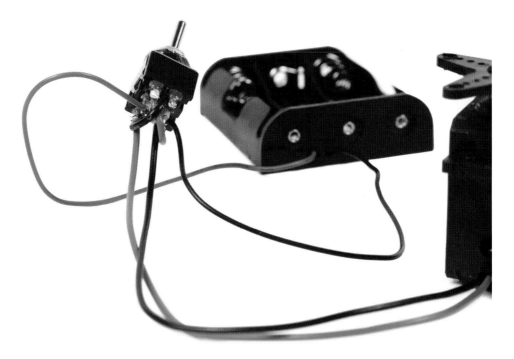

When the switch is toggled to make this connection, the black wire from the battery pack is connected to the red wire from the motor, and the red wire from the battery pack gets connected to the black wire from the motor. By crisscrossing the wires, you have effectively flipped the power supply to the motor when the switch is toggled.

The H-bridge A1 and A2 connections are the first set of terminals connected directly to the motor. The B1 and B2 connections on the H-bridge are the other outer terminals where the crisscrossed wires are connected when the switch is flipped.

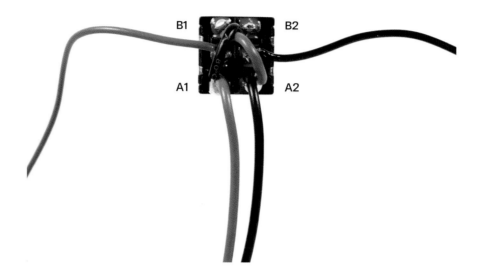

ADJUSTING THE MOTOR'S SPEED

Now that you understand how to adjust the motor's direction, you'll adjust its speed. Although there are many ways to control motor speed, the easiest method is to change the amount of voltage you are applying. The more voltage you apply to a motor, the faster it spins.

However, if you apply too much voltage, the coils inside the motor will overheat, the protective coating on the coils will melt, the wires will short, and the motor will stop working. Therefore, it is important to know what the maximum voltage rating is for a motor so that you don't overheat it and release the "magic smoke."

If you don't know what the operating voltage is, you can guess using the very scientific method of trial and error. Start with a small voltage supply of 3 V and gradually increase the amount of electricity. If either the motor or batteries get so hot that you can't touch them, you're giving the motor too much voltage. Let things cool down and use the previous power supply that you tested before it began to heat up.

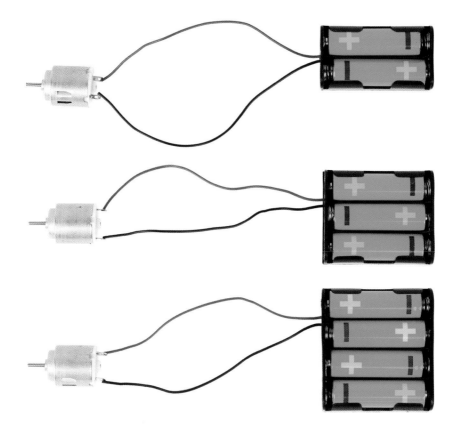

Although you can change the speed of the motor by applying more or less power, a better way to change the output speed of a motor is to use an additional gearbox. Many motors come with gearboxes attached to speed up or slow down the output speed.

Motor   Gearbox

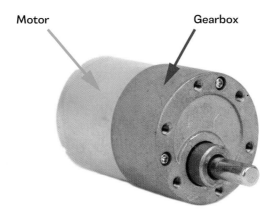

Servo Motors

A *servo motor* is a type of geared motor that has an electronic controller board inside. You can use a circuit board called a *microcontroller* (a kind of minicomputer) to talk to its controller board and control its rotation.

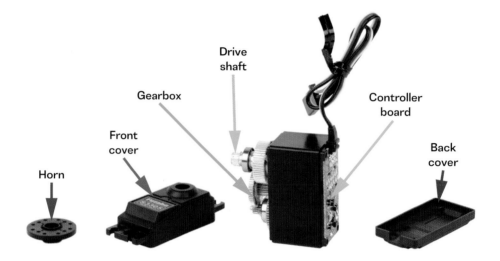

Drive shaft

Gearbox

Controller board

Front cover

Back cover

Horn

In this book, you'll be modifying servo motors to run off batteries without a microcontroller. To do this, you'll remove the controller board and connect a power and ground wire directly to the motor. You'll notice these servos have only two colored wires coming out of them instead of three.

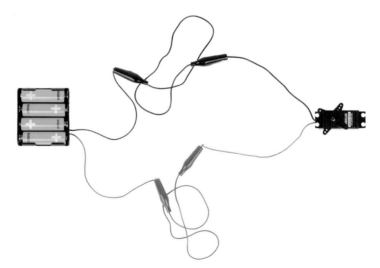

NOTE I can't stress this enough: while the servos in this book look normal, they are modified to work directly off batteries! To learn more, see Chapter 4.

However, before you start modifying the servos, it is important to understand a few things about them. First, while they look nearly identical, there is a big difference between a standard servo and a continuous servo.

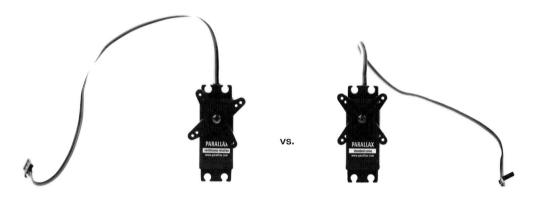

VS.

A *standard servo* cannot rotate in a full circle. A microcontroller is necessary to send the servo a signal that tells it to rotate to a certain position, usually some value between 0° and 180°. In fact, there is even a physical stop inside the gearbox that prevents the drive shaft from making a complete rotation.

| 180° | 135° | 45° | 0° |

Continuous servos can spin in full, continuous circles (hence the name). They cannot be told to travel to a particular degree around the circle. Instead of controlling the servo's specific position, the microcontroller is used to send a signal that controls the speed at which the servo rotates. Since a continuous-rotation servo does not have a physical stop in the gearbox, it's the best type of servo for you to remove the controller board and modify to run directly off a battery pack.

Servos come in a range of sizes. The most common size of servo, and the one you'll use throughout this book, is "standard" size. Don't confuse standard-size servos with standard *operation* servos. You'll exclusively be using a standard-size servo that operates in continuous rotation.

Some continuous-rotation servos also come in micro size. Those servos are too weak to work on the projects in this book. They're small (not much bigger than a quarter) and often come in a clear blue case.

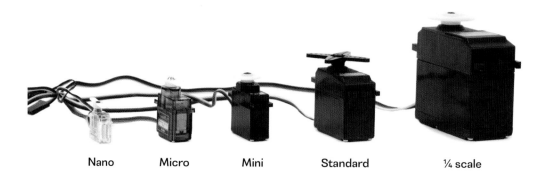

Nano   Micro   Mini   Standard   ¼ scale

You may be wondering why you're going to be modifying a servo instead of just buying a geared DC motor.

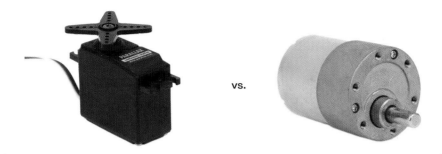

vs.

For starters, hobby servos operate in the range of 3 V to 6 V and can easily be powered by common battery packs ranging from 2 × AA to 4 × AA batteries.

Standard continuous-rotation servos always tend to be the same size and always have the same mounting tabs. This makes them universal to build with and easily attachable to other objects without the need for specialized mounting hardware.

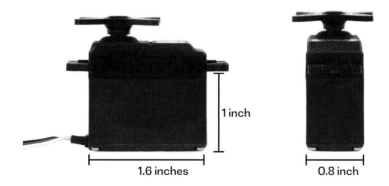

The servo also has a part that attaches to its rotating shaft called a *horn*. The many different horn shapes and attachments for servo motors make it easy to fasten items to the servo's rotating shaft. Zip-tying something to a servo horn is infinitely easier than attaching something to the rotating shaft of a generic geared DC motor.

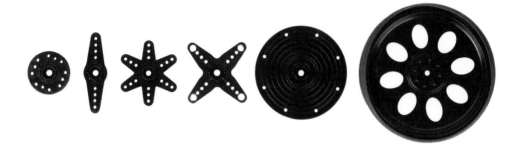

Nonmodified servos are used in more advanced robotics with microcontrollers. Because all standard-size servo motors are uniform in size and have the same mounting holes, it's easy to later swap out the servos and convert the robots made in this book so they can be controlled by a microcontroller like an Arduino.

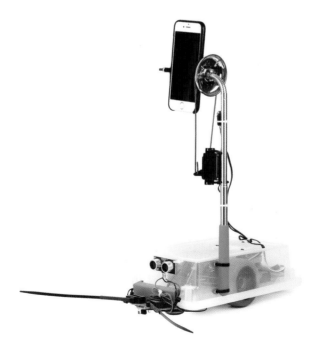

The one downside to modified servos is that they can be a pain in the neck to modify if you are new to electronics, but you'll gain all the necessary skills to do it when you learn to solder in the next chapter. Unfortunately, as of the time of writing this, it is difficult to find premodified controllerless servo motors for sale.

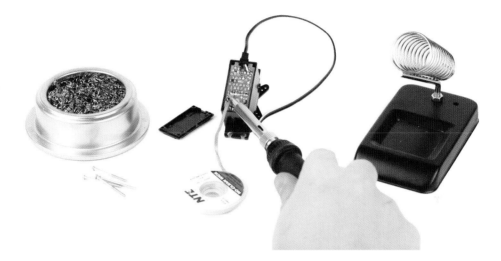

Should you not want to modify a servo and prefer to use a geared motor, some alternatives exist, but they all require some degree of improvisation to work with the projects in this book. While it might seem slightly easier or cheaper than modifying a servo, you'll discover that the amount of effort necessary to make these motors work is actually fairly high.

Nevertheless, you can find some ways to produce workable alternatives to the modified servo motors in Appendix A.

4

SOLDERING AND DESOLDERING

S older is a fusible metal alloy used to make permanent
electrical connections between wires and other electronic components. If you really want to dive deep into
robotics, eventually you'll need to learn to solder. By using solder
that melts under relatively low temperatures of a few hundred
degrees, you can join two pieces of metal together and create an
electrical bond. This requires both a particular set of tools and a
number of safety precautions.

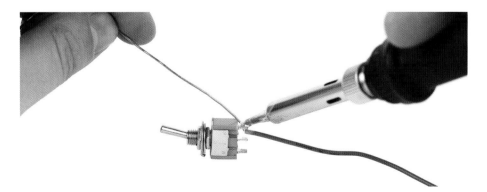

Soldering Tools and Materials

You'll need a number of basic items before soldering. First is a soldering iron. Although you can spend hundreds of dollars on a fancy soldering iron, a $15 adjustable iron (rated for about 60 W) should suffice to get started.

Once you have a soldering iron, you'll need a heatproof stand on which to rest the soldering iron when you are not using it. Most soldering irons typically come with a stand, but if yours does not, you absolutely need to purchase one.

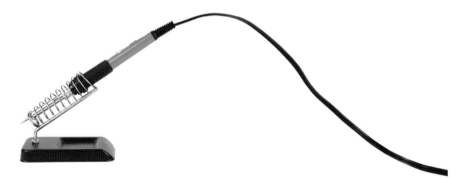

A cleaning pad is also necessary for cleaning the tip of the soldering iron after each use. Two commonly available options are wire pads, which tend to last longer, and slightly dampened sponges, which you should be able to find around your house. Use whichever you prefer.

You'll also need some solder. I highly recommend getting a roll of lead-free solder. It melts at a slightly higher temperature than lead solder and is a bit harder to work with, but it's not as toxic to handle. At the end of the day, your health should take priority over ease of use.

Desoldering braid, for undoing soldering mistakes, is another essential item for the projects in this book. It is also critical for removing solder from the circuit board inside of servo motors in order to detach the circuit from the motor itself, which is an action you'll need to take repeatedly when building these bots.

Finally, you should get a fume extractor fan to remove soldering fumes and protect your lungs. When melted, solder releases nasty fumes that you should avoid breathing in. It is best to use a filtered exhaust fan while soldering. At the very least, solder in a place with decent airflow blowing away from you to prevent the exhaust fumes from lingering.

Getting Started

Before you plug in your soldering iron, it is important to understand how to handle it safely when it is powered up. Hold the soldering iron much in the same way as you would hold a pencil, but with a very important exception. Instead of grasping the soldering iron near the tip, your hand should always grasp the insulated handle.

WARNING Never touch the metal part of the soldering iron with your hands when it is plugged in. It will be as hot (or hotter) than the surface of an oven and can seriously burn you.

Once you have a grasp on that, place the soldering iron in its holder, plug it in, and wait a few minutes for it to heat up to a temperature hot enough to melt solder. You can test that it's ready simply by touching the tip to some solder and seeing if it melts. If it does, you are ready to begin soldering. Also, while you are at it, turn on your exhaust fan, and make sure that you have the solder and soldering iron cleaning pad on hand.

The first time you use the soldering iron, you'll want to *tin* the tip. This means melting a coating of solder around the surface of the tip to coat it and keep it working well.

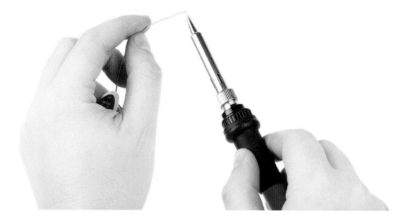

Melt solder all over the surface of the soldering iron tip until it has a nice, shiny silver coating. This will protect the metal tip from oxidizing and allow it to melt solder easily.

SOLDERING WIRES

The best way to practice soldering is to solder two wires together. Strip the ends off of two sections of wire and twist or hook the metallic ends together. Next, heat up the metal ends of the wires while pushing a piece of solder into the joint. The solder should liquify and spread over the joint, fusing the two together. If done correctly, the joint should look silver and shiny without any black patches or bulbous bits of solder protruding from it.

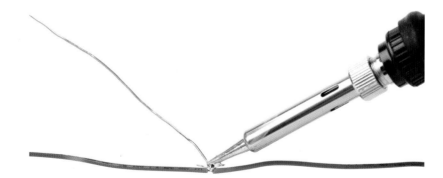

After you have effectively soldered the two pieces of wire together, clean the tip of the soldering iron by dragging it across the cleaning pad two or three times until the excess solder is removed.

If your solder connection is gray, black, bulbous, or feels rough in texture when cooled, you have created a *cold solder joint* by not sufficiently heating up the wires you are soldering together. You'll likely need to redo it. The easiest way is to trim the wires and start over.

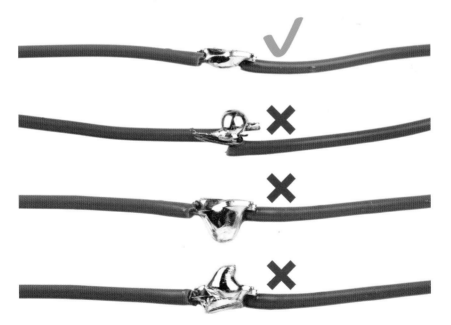

WARNING Don't ignore bad solder connections, because they can cause your circuit not to work; even worse, they can cause mysterious intermittent problems that will be difficult to figure out.

The last thing to consider is that it's best practice to insulate the wire connection. This helps prevent short circuits and other unwanted errors. The best way to do this is to use shrink tube to cover the solder joints.

Keep in mind that you'll need to slide the shrink tube on the wire *prior* to soldering the wire together, and then you'll position it once the wires are soldered. Finally, you'll want to shrink it using a heat gun so it fits snugly around the solder connection.

A heat gun is basically a turbocharged hair dryer that gets very, very hot. You need to be careful to point it away from you; otherwise, you could burn yourself. You also need to be careful not to point it at anything that might accidentally catch on fire (like paper).

Aside from soldering wires together, you can solder wires to components, such as motor terminals and switches. You can also solder components and wires directly to circuit boards, such as the components inside the servo motor.

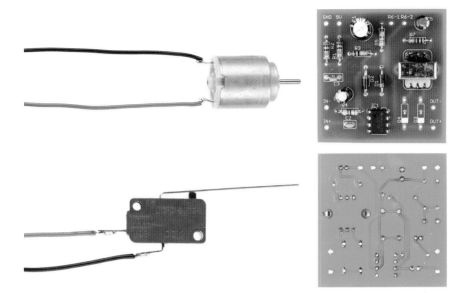

DESOLDERING

If you mess up and solder the wrong things together, you can use desoldering braid to remove solder and separate parts. To desolder, unwind some desoldering braid from its spool and lay it flat on the soldering connection you want to undo. Next, press down on the desoldering braid with your soldering iron until the solder starts to melt and be absorbed into the braid.

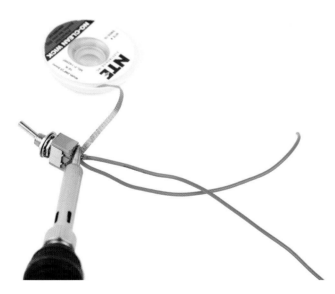

This is a little bit tricky and takes some practice to get right, but you're about to get a bit of practice doing this as you begin to modify a servo for direct drive.

Modifying the Servo for Direct Drive

As you start building bots, you'll find yourself repeating these steps often. At least one modified servo is called for with every bot in this book. You may find the desoldering process frustrating at times, but stick with it. The more you do it, the easier it will become.

Open the servo motor by removing the four screws holding the servo's back lid on and then removing the lid.

Unwind a few inches of desoldering braid from its spool.

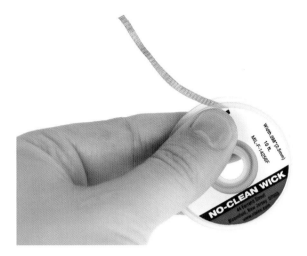

Locate the two solder connections for the DC motor on the servo's circuit board. These connections will be the two largest blobs of solder on one end of the circuit board. Often there will be a cutaway in the circuit board itself, and you might even be able to see a little bit of the metal motor casing.

Place the desoldering braid over the motor's solder joints.

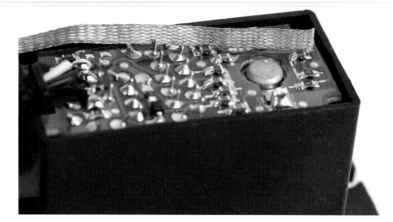

Press down on top of the desoldering braid with your soldering iron until you see and/or feel the solder beneath the braid start to liquify and flow. You'll see the desoldering braid around the tip of the soldering iron begin to turn silver.

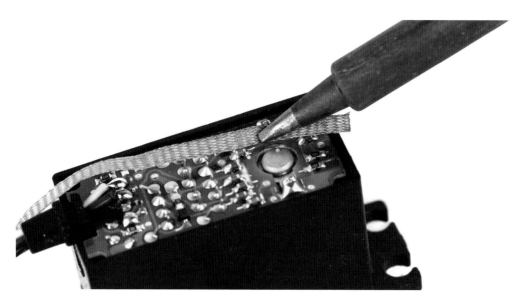

Once the desoldering braid has started turning silver, count to two and simultaneously lift away the soldering iron and the desoldering braid by gripping its packaging (and not the exposed metal braid).

WARNING The desoldering braid is hot, so be careful handling it until it has cooled.

On the braid, you should now see a shiny solder blob. If all went well, most of the blob of solder on the circuit board will now be gone, and the circuit board will be detached from the motor pin. If solder is still attaching the motor pin to the circuit board, simply repeat the process until the motor pin has been completely desoldered from the board. Repeat this same process for the second motor pin.

Once both pins have been freed, remove the circuit board from the body of the servo.

Now you can practice your soldering skills. To begin, cut a red wire and black wire to 6 inches in length and then strip ½ inch of insulation off the end of each. Next, apply a light coat of solder to the end of each wire.

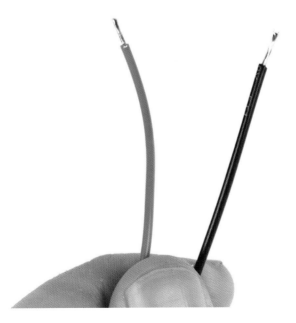

This is called *tinning*, just as you did with the soldering iron tip earlier. You do this because solder really likes to stick to other solder. Since the motor pins already have a little solder on them, applying a little bit of solder to each wire makes it much easier to connect the wires and pins together.

Place the red wire against the motor pin closest to the red dot on the back of the motor. If your motor doesn't have a red dot, pick a side of the servo motor to be designated the "left side" and always attach your red wires to that side.

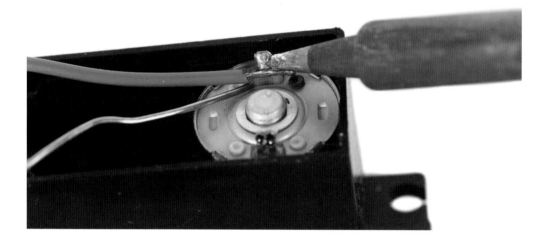

Once that is squared away, carefully apply the soldering iron to the joint where the wire and pin meet and melt a little bit of solder into it. You should see the solder start to liquify and spread over both. When this happens, remove the soldering iron and solder and then wait for the solder joint to cool and solidify before handling it.

 NOTE Don't forget to clean the tip of the soldering iron.

Repeat this process using the black wire and the other motor pin.

Tie the motor's wires in a knot such that the knot would be located outside of the servo's enclosure should you pull on the cord. Once you are sure of this, place the knot inside of the servo's enclosure. Having this knot inside the servo will prevent the motor's wires from becoming detached from the motor pin if you pull on them.

Reassemble the servo and reinsert the screws holding it together.

Your servo is now able to be powered directly from batteries. To make it spin, simply connect each wire from your servo to the power wire with the same color coming from a battery pack.

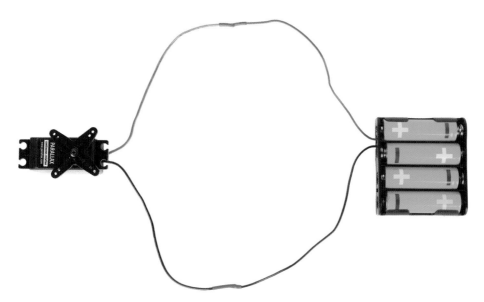

WARNING Be sure to unplug the soldering iron when you are finished with it.

While soldering and desoldering are necessary skills for advancing in robotics, if you are not quite ready to try them, you can build entire circuits without any soldering at all. To discover alternatives for making electrical connections without soldering, check out Appendix A.

5

WOBBLER

As you likely guessed from the name, Wobbler is a bot that moves around by wobbling back and forth. While it might seem a little clumsy initially, don't let first impressions fool you. Wobbler is an enthusiastic and persistent little bot ready to take on the world.

The parts for this project are all easy to find, and the Wobbler should be straightforward to put together, even for less-experienced bot builders. More-experienced bot builders will have some fun modifying this one, as the design's simplicity leaves a lot of room for expansion and experimentation.

Tools and Supplies

- Two continuous-rotation servo motors with the controllers removed
- Two self-adhesive oval coat hooks
- A 4 × AA battery holder
- Four AA batteries
- Small plastic container with lid
- Four zip ties
- Marker
- Wire stripper/cutting pliers
- Power drill
- A ⅛-inch drill bit
- A ⅜-inch or ½-inch drill bit

Wobbler Overview

You'll build Wobbler in stages. First, you need to have premodified the continuous-rotation servo motors for direct drive (Chapter 4) or sourced one of the geared motor alternatives as outlined in Appendix A. Once that's complete, you'll mark and drill the plastic box to mount the motors, attach the motors inside the box, and wire up the circuit. Finally, you'll mount Wobbler's oval "wheels" on the outside of the box.

Constructing Wobbler

Step 1. Remove the servo horns from the motors. (A servo horn is the part attached to the motor shaft that spins.)

Step 2. Place the servos inside the plastic container such that they're mirrored back to back. The servo shafts where the horns used to be should be located near the bottom of the plastic container and a little off-center to help Wobbler wobble.

Step 1

Step 3. Mark the plastic container with a marker over the mounting screw holes and the motors' shafts to indicate their positions.

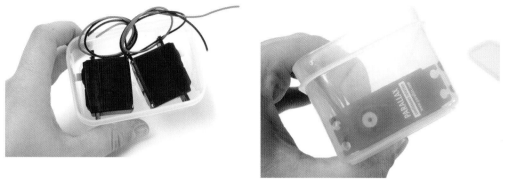

Step 2   Step 3

Step 4. Drill holes in the plastic container where you made the marks.

Step 4

For the smaller mounting holes, a ⅛-inch drill bit should be suitable. For the motor shaft, use either a ⅜-inch or ½-inch drill bit.

Step 5. Position the motors inside the plastic container and zip-tie them securely in place.

Step 5

Step 6. Connect a red wire from one of the motors to a black wire from the other motor. Connect the paired wires with one of the wires from the battery holder. Next, connect together the remaining three loose wires to form another grouping. You can either solder these wires or use a mechanical connector.

Step 6

Step 7. Place the battery holder inside the plastic container. Then close the plastic container and reattach the servo horns.

Step 8. Although this step isn't entirely necessary, take the coat hooks and trim off the hook part with diagonal cutting pliers or a small saw. You'll be left with self-adhesive oval wheels.

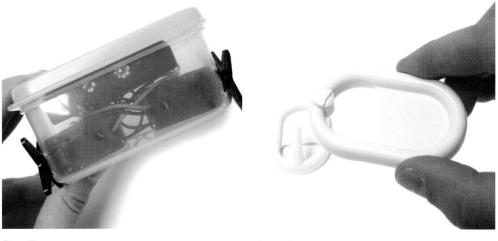

Step 7

Step 8

Step 9. Peel off the adhesive backing and stick the wheels to the servo horns such that each horn is completely hidden behind its wheel. Make sure to stick the wheels so they're very off-center from the axis of rotation to give the bot a good wobble.

Step 9

Step 10. Remove the lid, insert batteries into the battery holder, close the lid again, and let Wobbler go. The robot will keep going so long as the batteries are installed.

> **NOTE** Be sure to remove the batteries to turn the bot off. See Appendix A for instructions on adding a power switch.

Step 10

Experiment with setting the bot on different sides to observe all the ways it moves. Also try replacing the coat hook "wheels" with other objects to get unique results. Simply attach different objects to the servo horn with double-sided tape or zip ties.

6

BUFFER

Buffer is very similar to Wobbler in many regards, but the main difference is its wheels. For this bot, you'll attach two round "buffer" wheels to downward-facing motors that are rotating toward each other, so when you turn the bot on, it propels itself in the direction the scrubbers are spinning. Buffer looks a bit like a tiny street sweeper, but it moves differently from its larger cousin. However, it may actually clean your floor. Buffer is an easy little bot to build and fun to use.

Tools and Supplies

- Two continuous-rotation servo motors with the controllers removed
- A 4 × AA battery holder
- Lid from a 12-inch plastic rectangular container
- Two dryer lint—catching brushes
- Two stainless-steel plumbing flange repair rings
- A 24-inch aluminum ruler
- Four ¼- inch nuts and bolts
- Two 4-40 × ¼-inch nuts and bolts
- Zip ties of assorted sizes
- Power drill
- Three drill bits: ⅛, ¼, and ½ inch
- Hacksaw
- Wire stripper/cutting pliers
- Marker

Buffer Overview

First, you'll modify the servos, just like you did with Wobbler (see also Chapter 4) or use one of the geared motor alternatives from Appendix A. Once this is completed, you'll build the lint-brush buffer wheels. Then, you'll attach the motors to the box lid and the buffing wheels to the motors, face-down toward the ground. Finally, you'll wire together and power up the whole circuit.

Constructing Buffer

Step 1. Prepare the crossbars for Buffer's brush wheels. You'll use these crossbars to attach the servo horn to the wheel itself. Cut the ruler into two 7-inch sections, which should be the diameter of the stainless-steel plumbing flange repair rings.

Step 1

Step 2. You're going to drill holes into the sections of ruler to attach those ruler sections to the repair ring and begin making Buffer's wheels. First, position one ruler section across your repair ring, and with a marker pen, mark the ruler through the repair ring's mounting holes at both ends of the ruler piece, as shown here. Try to get the mark as near to the center of the ruler's width as possible. Repeat with the second section of the ruler.

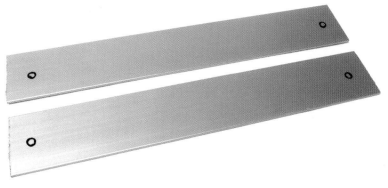

Step 2

Step 3. Firmly clamp down the ruler sections, drill ⅛-inch pilot holes into the marks on them, and then widen the holes to ¼ inch.

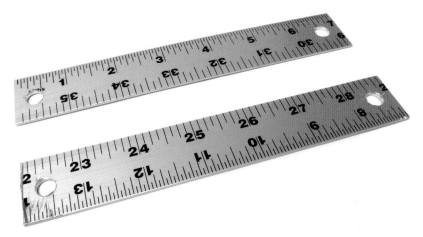

Step 3

Step 4. Remove the screws attaching the servo horns to the servo motors and pull the horns off the motor boxes.

Step 5. Drill ⅛-inch holes through the ends of each servo horn.

Step 4   Step 5

Step 6. Align a servo horn with the center of one ruler section. Two of the holes you previously drilled into the servo horn should hang over the edges of the ruler. Mark the ruler through the other two holes you previously drilled into the servo horn. Do the same for the other ruler section.

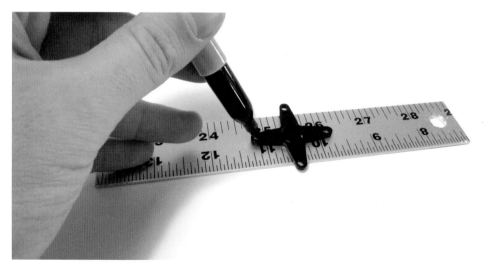

Step 6

Step 7. Using a ⅛-inch drill bit, drill holes where you just marked each section of ruler.

Step 7

Step 8. Using your ¼-inch nuts and bolts, fasten each ruler section to a repair ring through the larger holes you drilled.

Step 8

Step 9. Chop the handles off your lint-catching brushes.

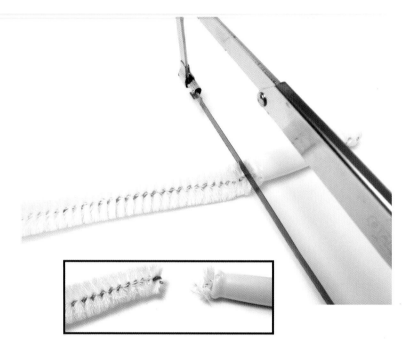

Step 9

Step 10. To complete Buffer's wheels, bend a lint brush around the bottom face of a repair ring so it forms a circle, zip-tying it in place as you go. Cut off excess zip-tie leads and any extra lint brush that remains. Repeat the process for the second lint brush and repair ring.

Step 10

Step 11. Take the plastic box lid and mark it about ¾ inch in from each of the shorter edges of the lid. Try to get the marks in the center. Drill a ½-inch hole where you placed your two marks. If the plastic cracks or chips a little, it's okay, so long as you can still zip-tie the motor in place.

Step 11

Step 12. Now you'll add holes to mount the servo motors with zip ties. Position the servo motor shaft into the center of one of the holes you just drilled. Make a mark on the lid over each of the four servo-mounting holes. Repeat this process for the other hole you drilled. Finally, drill holes through these eight marks using a ⅛-inch drill bit.

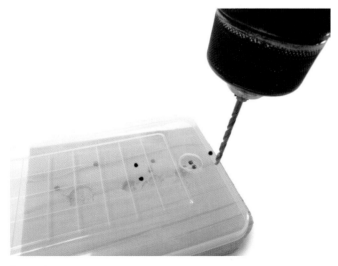

Step 12

Step 13. Through these holes, zip-tie the motors to the box lid such that the lid's lip points in the opposite direction of the motor shafts.

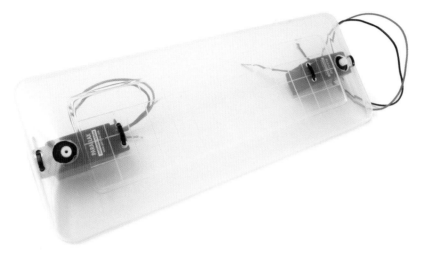

Step 13

Step 14. Now position the battery holder on the center of the lid and mark the lid through the battery holder's two mounting holes. Drill through these marks using a ⅛-inch drill bit.

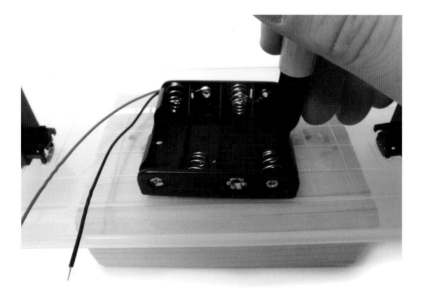

Step 14

Step 15. Fasten the battery holder to the same side of the lid as your motors with the 4-40 × ¼-inch nuts and bolts.

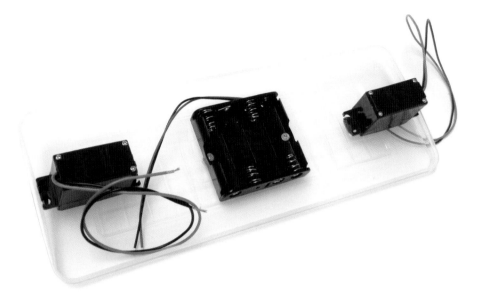

Step 15

Step 16. Reattach the servo horns to the servos.

Step 16

Step 17. Zip-tie the buffer wheels to the servo horns through the mounting holes you drilled earlier. For each wheel and servo-horn pair, pass a zip tie down through the servo horn and a hole in the ruler, then back up through one of the holes in the servo horn that sticks off the edge of the ruler, and then tie the zip tie. Repeat this process with the second zip tie, and make sure everything is firmly secured. Trim all excess zip-tie leads.

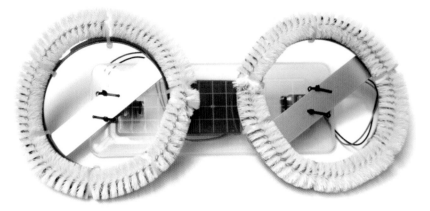

Step 17

Step 18. Connect the red wire from one servo to the black wire on the other servo. Connect the remaining two black and red servo wires together. Attach one of these pairs to the red wire of the battery pack. Attach the other pair to the black wire. Zip-tie all of the wires neatly together, making certain that none of the exposed solder joints can touch each other and short the bot. Alternatively, insulate the connections with shrink tube.

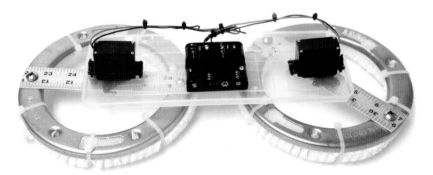

Step 18

Step 19. Insert some batteries into the battery holder, put Buffer down, and watch it go!

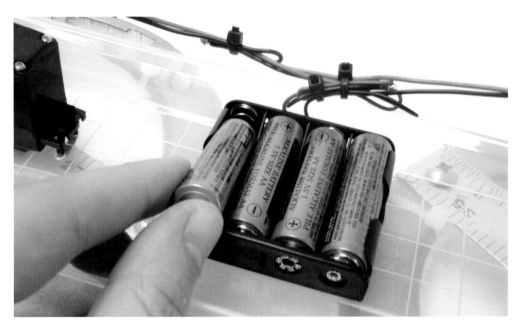

Step 19

> ➡ **NOTE** Be sure to remove the batteries to turn the bot off. See Appendix A for instructions on adding a power switch.

DAZE

aze is an unusual bot for a few reasons. First, its wheels are also its body. Second, its movement mechanisms are made of two servos with the motor shafts connected together off-center. This began as an experiment, and I would never have guessed this bot would move the way it does. At any given time, Daze might decide to roll forward, backward, or simply stay in place. It's almost as if the bot is moving around in a daze—hence, the name.

Tools and Supplies

- Two continuous-rotation servo motors with the controllers removed
- Two 3 × AA battery holders
- Six AA batteries
- Two CDs or DVDs
- Four 4-40 × ⅜-inch nuts and bolts
- Cutting template (see Appendix B)
- Zip ties of assorted sizes
- Scissors
- Roll of painter's tape (or similar)
- Power drill
- A ⅛-inch drill bit
- Wire stripper/cutting pliers

Daze Overview

You'll build Daze using the same modified servo motors (Chapter 4) or geared motor alternatives (Appendix A) you used for the other bots. Daze consists of two identical halves that are attached off-center to each other. You'll start by using the drilling template to modify the CDs (or DVDs) that will act as the bot's wheels. Next, you'll attach the motors and the battery packs to the wheels and then attach the servo horns together (off-center). Finally, you'll wire each motor to its own battery pack and power up Daze.

Constructing Daze

Step 1. Print out a copy of the template sheet from *https://nostarch .com/homemaderobots/* (or trace it from Appendix B) and cut out both of the round drilling templates.

Step 2. Center and tape a drilling template to each CD.

Step 1

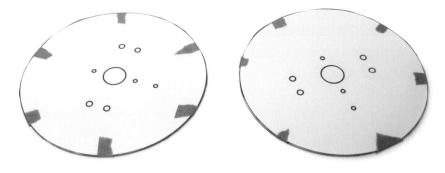

Step 2

Step 3. Drill the holes indicated by the template using a ⅛-inch drill bit.

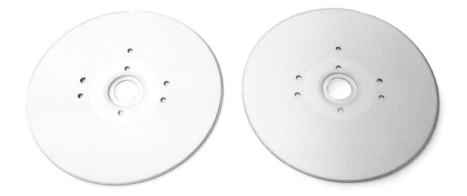

Step 3

Step 4. Take the horns off the servo motors. On one of the arms of each servo horn, drill two ⅛-inch holes: one near the tip of the horn and one near the base. Drill identical holes on the other horn. Reattach the horns to the servo motors.

Step 4

Step 5. For each CD and servo pair, lay the CD flat and place the servo on top of the center of the CD, with the horn away from the CD. Line up the CD's four holes with the servo's mounting holes and then zip-tie the servo to the CD. Trim away the zip tie's tail.

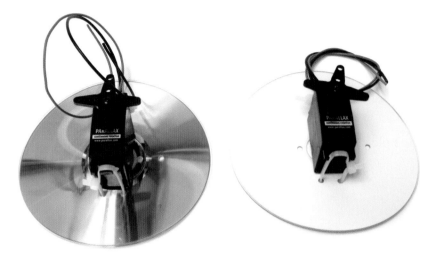

Step 5

Step 6. Use nuts and bolts to attach the battery holders to the sides of the CDs opposite the servos.

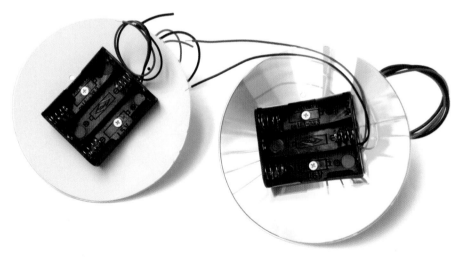

Step 6

Step 7. Zip-tie the servo horns together through the four holes you drilled earlier. Pull the zip tie tight, trim away the excess, and make sure the servo horns can both spin unimpeded.

Step 8. Pass both servo motor wires through the one remaining unused hole in each CD, toward the battery holder.

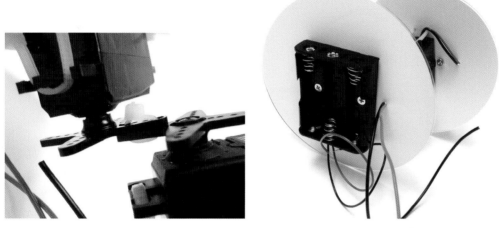

Step 7   Step 8

Step 9. On one of the CDs, connect the red motor wire together with the red battery wire and the black motor wire with the black battery wire. On the other CD, connect the red motor wire to the black battery wire and the black motor wire to the red battery wire, such that it's wired opposite to the first.

Step 9

Step 10. Zip-tie everything tightly together, eliminating the slack so that the solder joints can't possibly touch and result in a short circuit.

Step 11. To make Daze go, place it on a surface where it cannot fall, insert batteries into each battery holder, and then watch in wonder.

Step 10   Step 11

> **NOTE** Be sure to remove the batteries to turn the bot off. See Appendix A for instructions on adding power switches.

8

BARRELLER

Barreller Bot has seemingly eternal forward propulsion in a given direction. Put simply, it has a motor that acts as an off-centered weight inside a can. When gravity pulls the weight (that is, the motor) down, the can rolls forward. A normal can would likely stop rolling at that point, but this can has a tilt switch that turns the motor on when it drops, causing the motor to rotate back upward (and turn off again), which restarts the process. If you can imagine

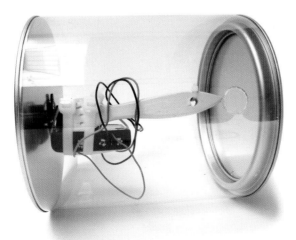

this happening really quickly and for a sustained amount of time, you'll understand what this bot does. The Barreller has the appearance of rolling forward on its own and even doing seemingly impossible things like rolling up inclines. This bot is great fun. If you don't believe me, build one for yourself. It's quick and easy to do.

Tools and Supplies

- Continuous-rotation servo motor with the controller removed
- Paint can (or similar)
- Two 1-inch paintbrushes
- A 4 × AA battery holder
- Four AA batteries
- Tilt switch (Mouser #107-2002-EV)
- Assorted zip ties
- Drilling template (see Appendix B)

Barreller Overview

The Barreller is built inside a paint can (I used a clear novelty can). Before you do anything, make sure you have modified the continuous servo motor for direct drive (Chapter 4) or are using one of the geared motor alternatives, as outlined in Appendix A. Once that is complete, the next step is building the inner "weight" mechanism, which is essentially a circuit consisting of a motor, battery pack, and tilt switch. You'll insert this mechanism into the can and attach it to the center.

Constructing Barreller

Step 1. Take apart both paintbrushes such that you are left with the two wooden handles.

Step 1

Step 2. Put batteries into the battery holder and lay it down on top of a zip tie with the batteries facing down. Place the motor on top of the battery holder so that the servo horn sticks off perpendicularly in one direction and the wooden handles are sticking off in the opposite direction. Zip-tie everything firmly together until it is one singular unit and won't pull apart.

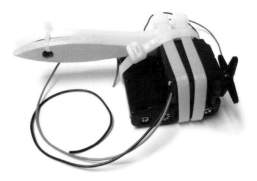

Step 2

Step 3. Twist together the black wire from the motor with the black wire from the battery holder and solder the connection. Solder the red wire from the battery holder to the little spike that sticks out of the tilt switch. Solder the red wire from the motor to the conductive metallic shell of the tilt switch. When the tilt switch is activated, electricity will flow between the spike and the outer shell.

Step 3

> **NOTE** It's easier to solder to the tilt switch if you place a small pool of solder on it first. Some newer tilt switches even have two wires and don't require soldering a wire to the outer shell.

Step 4. Prepare the can by removing anything that will prevent it from rolling, such as handles, and clean out anything that may be inside.

Step 5. Print (or trace) and cut out the template. Tape the template to the bottom of the can and drill the four smaller holes with a ⅛-inch drill bit or one appropriately sized for your zip ties.

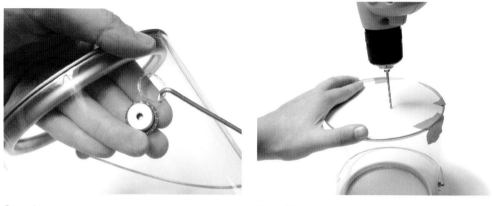

Step 4   Step 5

Step 6. Slip the tilt switch between two of the batteries in the battery holder such that it is parallel with them. However, make certain this doesn't short out the switch. If you are concerned about this, you can cover it with shrink tube (not pictured).

Step 7. Widen the holes in the servo horn using a ⅛-inch drill bit such that they match the holes drilled in the bottom of the can.

Step 6   Step 7

Step 8. Zip-tie the servo horn to the holes you drilled in the bottom of the can. Trim the zip tie tails.

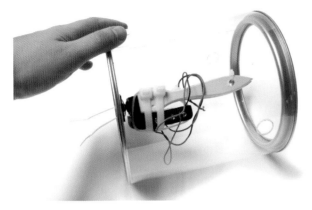

Step 8

Step 9. Put the lid back on when you are done.

Step 9

 NOTE If you tilt Barreller on its side, it'll roll indefinitely until it collides with something. Store the can upright (in its normal position) to keep the bot from turning on.

9

LAZY

As its name implies, Lazy Bot has been optimized to do very little. This is a design feature and not a bug. Once a minute, Lazy Bot lurches forward and then comes to a stop. This works thanks to a magnet-activated reed switch and a small magnet attached to the second hand of a clock. When the clock's second hand with the magnet passes over the reed switch, the bot turns on for just a few seconds. In this way, Lazy

Bot is highly effective at the task it has been assigned. I can envision a day in the not-so-distant future when robots become even more competent at slacking off than people.

Tools and Supplies

- Two continuous-rotation servo motors with the controllers removed
- Two 1½-inch putty knives
- Round wall clock
- Reed switch
- Hacksaw
- Small disc magnet
- Shrink tube
- A 3 × AA battery holder
- Three AA batteries
- Assorted zip ties

Lazy Overview

Lazy Bot is made from a simple circuit built around the body of a clock. Before you start building it, make sure you have modified the continuous servo motor for direct drive (Chapter 4) or are using one of the geared motor alternatives, as outlined in Appendix A. The next step is to take apart the clock face and set aside all the pieces. Once you can access the inside of the clock without obstructions, you'll attach the reed switch and batteries. You'll then modify the clock's body so you can attach the motors and their arms. After all of the components are in place, you'll be able to complete the wiring of the circuit. The last major step will be attaching a magnet to the second hand and reinstalling it inside the body of the clock. You can then put the clock's protective cover back on if you like.

Constructing Lazy

Step 1. Remove the front cover from the clock. Carefully remove the clock hands from the movement (clock mechanism) and then remove the clock face.

Step 1

Step 2. Attach a red wire to the center terminal of the reed switch and a black wire to the outer common terminal.

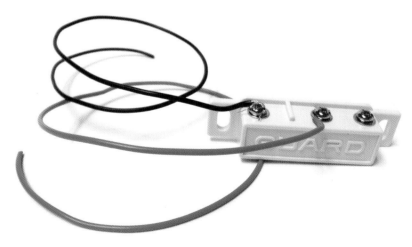

Step 2

Step 3. Zip-tie the reed switch to the inside of the clock, such that it is strapped around the clock movement case and the terminals are facing down.

Step 4. Find a place to secure the battery holder on the inside of the clock body. Make marks on each side of the battery holder so that when you drill holes, you'll be able to zip-tie the battery holder to the clock. Also, mark an extra hole through which you can pass the reed switch wires.

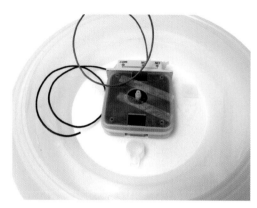 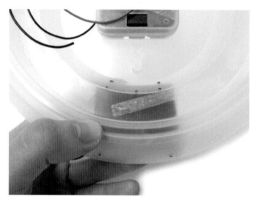

Step 3   Step 4

Step 5. Drill all of your marks with a ³⁄₁₆-inch drill bit.

Step 5

Step 6. Pass the wires from the reed switch through the extra hole you just marked and drilled. If possible, secure the wires by tying them around a part of the clock body or by tying them into a knot larger than the hole.

Step 7. Put batteries in the battery holder. You can optionally place a piece of tape over one of the wire leads until you are ready to use the wires. This will prevent the wires from crossing.

Step 6

Step 8. Zip-tie the battery holder to the clock body.

Step 9. Place the clock face back on the clock body. Make two marks on the outer body of the clock, between 2 and 3 o'clock, to indicate the width of the servo body. Make similar marks between 9 and 10 o'clock.

Step 7

Step 8

Step 9

Step 10. Where you made the marks, use a hacksaw and cut out two rectangles just large enough to pass the bodies of the servo motors through.

Step 11. With a hacksaw, trim away about 1½ inches from the scraper ends of the plastic putty knives. You should be left with just the handles.

Step 12. Remove the servo horns from the motor shafts and set the screws aside somewhere safe.

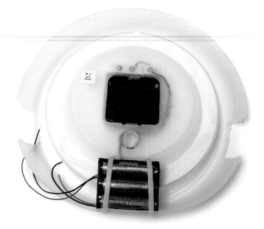

Step 10

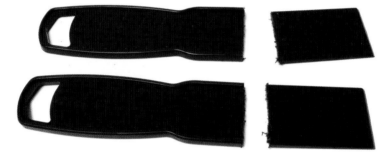

Step 11

Step 12

Step 13. Drill a ⅛-inch hole in each of the outer ends of the servo horn. Repeat on the other servo horn.

Step 13

Step 14. Use a servo horn as a drilling guide for making four mounting holes near the sawed-off edges of the plastic putty knives.

Step 15. Mount the servo horns back onto the motor shafts.

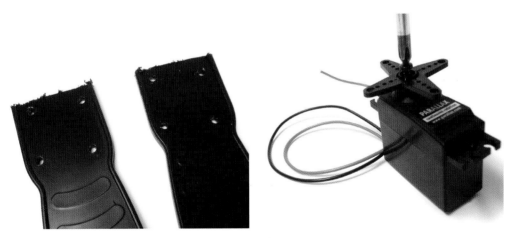

Step 14

Step 15

Step 16. Insert the servo motors into the holes you made in the side of the clock body. Use the servo mounting brackets as drilling guides to make mounting holes in the clock body.

Step 16

Step 17. Zip-tie the motors to the clock body, such that both of the servo horns are closer to 12 o'clock.

Step 18. Zip-tie the plastic putty knives to the servo horns.

Step 17   Step 18

Step 19. Attach your disc magnet to the underside of the clock's second hand with heat-shrink tubing in such a way that the magnet will pass over the reed switch when put back onto the clock movement. If you don't have heat-shrink tubing, a little piece of tape should do.

Step 19

Step 20. You can now remove the clock face again if you would like. More important, put the second hand back onto the clock movement.

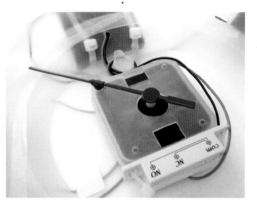

Step 20

Step 21. Solder the red wire from the reed switch to the red wire of the battery holder. Solder the black wire from the reed switch to the black wire from one of the servos and the red wire from the opposite servo.

Solder the black wire from the battery holder to the remaining two free servo wires.

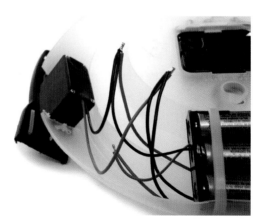

Step 21

Step 22. Zip-tie all the wires together so that the slack is pulled taut and none of the solder connections can cross.

Step 23. Put the front cover back onto the clock to protect the second hand.

Step 24. Insert a fresh (not partially drained) battery and wait. When the second hand passes over the reed switch, the bot will wake up for a moment and lurch its way into your heart.

Step 22

Step 23

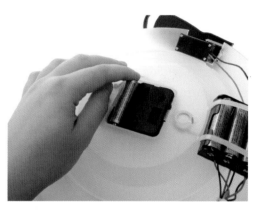

Step 24

➡️ **NOTE** Remove the clock battery when the second hand is not over the reed switch to turn the bot off. See Appendix A for instructions on adding a power switch.

10

SKITTER

A s the name suggests, Skitter Bot really likes to get around. Using just a single motor and a DPDT switch wired as an H-bridge, Skitter's feet shuffle back and forth to move it forward. This is perhaps one of the simplest and most reliable walking-type bots you might ever construct. It is designed to do only one thing, and it does it very well. In spite of having only a single purpose, one nice side effect of its scrub-brush feet is that it'll sweep your floor wherever it goes.

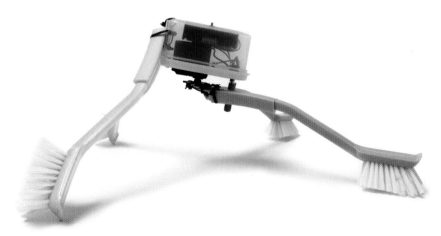

Tools and Supplies

- Continuous-rotation servo motor with the controller removed
- A 3 × AA battery holder
- Three AA batteries
- DPDT toggle switch
- Four scrub brushes (with long handles)
- Small plastic container (mine is 3½ × 2½ × 2 inches)
- BIC Round Stic pen
- A 1½ × ⅜-inch corner brace
- Drill
- ¼-inch and ⅛-inch drill bits
- Wire stripper
- Cutting pliers
- Box cutter
- Hot glue
- An assortment of zip ties

Skitter Overview

To build Skitter, you'll first modify a continuous-rotation servo for direct drive by removing its controller board (Chapter 4) or use one of the geared motor alternatives, as outlined in Appendix A. The next step is to attach two scrub brushes to the rear of the servo motor. You'll then mount the motor itself onto the lid of a plastic container. After that, you'll attach the battery to the plastic container itself and attach the remaining two scrub brushes to the front. You'll then fasten the DPDT switch to the lid and then wire the switch in an H-bridge configuration to complete the circuit. You'll extend the switch's lever with a tube from a pen so it can make contact with the oscillating scrub brushes. Finally, you'll insert the batteries and snap the lid shut to make the bot go.

Constructing Skitter

Step 1. Drill a ⅛-inch hole in each of the four ends of the servo horn.

Step 2. Choose two adjacent holes that you made in the servo horn and pass a zip tie down through each. Next, pass the zip ties through the

Step 1

two adjacent centermost holes in the corner brace. Then, pass the zip ties through the hanging holes in two of the brush handles. Finally, zip-tie everything firmly together.

Step 3. Use the two free holes in the corner brace as a guide for drilling downward through each of the brushes.

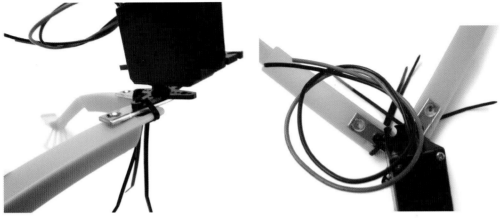

Step 2   Step 3

Step 4. Securely zip-tie the brushes to the corner brace using the holes you just drilled. For extra support, zip-tie the brush handle hanging holes to the unused back holes of the servo horn.

Step 4

Step 5. Center the backside of your servo near one of the short edges of the plastic container lid. Trace the outline of the back of the servo and then cut out the shape with a box cutter. Finally, pass the motor wires through the hole and slide the plastic container lid down over the servo.

Step 6. Drill ⅛-inch holes in the plastic container lid that line up with the servo's mounting holes.

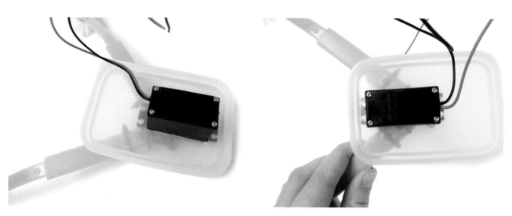

Step 5   Step 6

Step 7. Zip-tie the motor firmly in place, and trim away the excess.

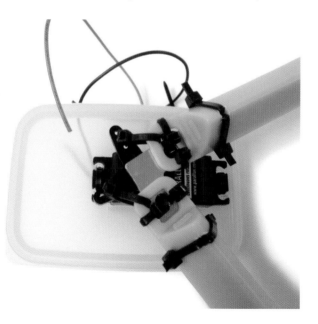

Step 7

Step 8. Center the battery holder over the underside of the plastic container and use the holder's mounting holes as a drill guide. Drill two ⅛-inch holes.

Step 9. Place the battery holder inside the plastic container and fasten the two items together using nuts and bolts.

Step 8

Step 9

Step 10. For each of the two remaining scrub brushes, measure 1 inch in from the end of the handle and make a mark. Drill a ⅛-inch hole down through the handle where you made this mark.

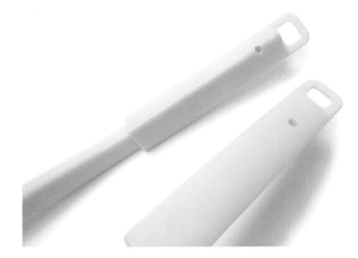

Step 10

Step 11. Turn the plastic container upside down. Mark, drill, and zip-tie the two remaining scrub brushes to the front of the plastic container such that they meet at a 90° angle and point evenly downward toward the direction of the plastic container opening. In other words, make two even-length front legs for your bot.

Step 12. Drill a ¼-inch centered hole near the short edge of the plastic container lid opposite the servo motor.

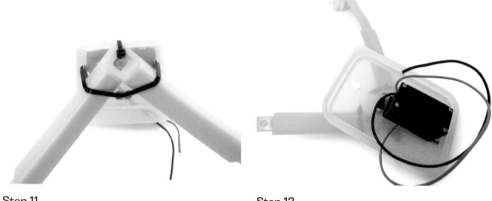

Step 11   Step 12

Step 13. Pass the DPDT switch through the hole so that the shaft is pointing at the scrub-brush legs, and then fasten the switch on with a nut.

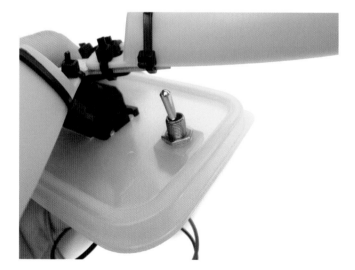

Step 13

Step 14. Wire together the opposite corners of the DPDT switch. Solder the red battery wire to one of the center DPDT switch pins and the black battery wire to the other.

Turn the switch so that there are only two pins facing you (as opposed to three). Solder the black motor wire to the DPDT pin closest to you on the right. Solder the red motor wire to the other pin on the left.

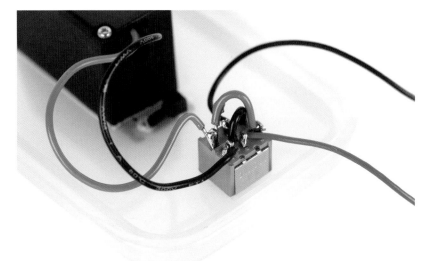

Step 14

> **NOTE** Refer to "H-Bridges" on page 30 in Chapter 3 for more information on how to change the direction that a motor is spinning using a switch.

Step 15. Take apart the BIC pen and cut about 1½ inches from the end of the pen tube to use it as an extender for the switch's lever.

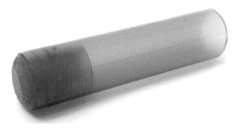

Step 15

Step 16. Make certain the switch is positioned between the two scrub brushes. Fill the pen cap with hot glue and, using pliers, quickly slide it onto the switch's shaft. Hold the hot tube in place until it begins to set. Be careful not to push it on too far; otherwise, you could get hot glue inside the switch, which could prevent it from working.

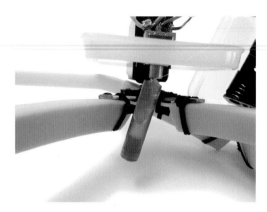

Step 16

Step 17. Put some batteries into the holder, and the legs will start to move.

Step 17

> ➡ **NOTE** If, when you power up the bot, the switch isn't making the legs oscillate back and forth, remove the batteries. Then, simply rotate the switch 180° in its mounting hole. It should now work perfectly when you reinsert the batteries.

Step 18. Quickly close the plastic container and let the bot go free.

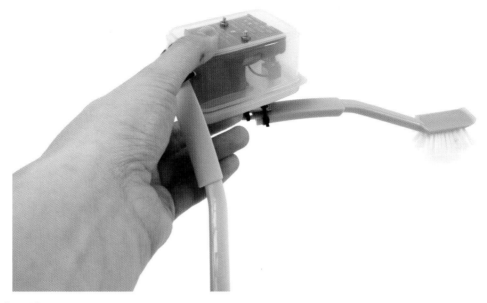

Step 18

> ➡ **NOTE** Be sure to remove the batteries to turn the bot off. See Appendix A for instructions on adding a power switch.

11

INCHWORM

If you can count on only one thing, it would be a ruler. Now, don't get me wrong. I'm not talking about supreme despots for life or anything of that sort. The rulers I'm referring to are the measuring kind. How can you not count on something with so many sequential numbers? That's why when deciding on the armature for Inchworm Bot, the only thing I could think

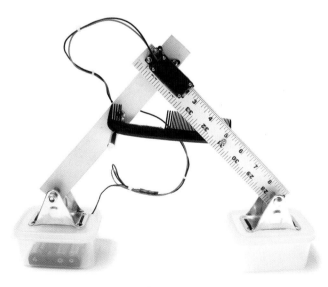

of was my good, dependable friend, the ruler. After all, "inch" is part of its name, and rulers are covered in inches. In addition, aluminum rulers make great robot parts. Not only are they structurally sound, they're also easy to cut, drill, and bend. Make your own Inchworm Bot to see for yourself.

Tools and Supplies

- Continuous-rotation servo motor with the controller removed
- Hacksaw
- A 4 × AA battery holder
- DPDT lever switch
- Four AA batteries
- Red and black wire
- Electrical tape
- An 18-inch aluminum ruler (or longer)
- Two small plastic containers, such as snack or baby food containers
- Two 2-inch fixed casters
- BIC Round Stic pen
- Cutting blade
- Comb

- Ten 4-40 × ½-inch nuts and bolts
- Four small washers
- A 2-inch metal standoff
- Four zip ties
- Wire stripper
- Cutting pliers
- Pliers
- Drill
- A ⅛-inch drill bit
- A ¼-inch drill bit
- A ³⁄₁₆-inch drill bit
- Hammer
- Bench vise
- Screwdriver
- 220-grit sandpaper
- Marker

Inchworm Overview

To make this bot, first modify a continuous-rotation servo for direct drive by removing its controller board (Chapter 4) or use one of the geared motor alternatives, as outlined in Appendix A. The next series of steps in building this bot involves cutting, bending, and drilling the ruler to create two distinct sections. You'll attach one section of the ruler to the body of the servo motor and the other ruler section to its horn. Once that's complete, you'll modify the comb to attach it to the ruler. Next, you'll attach the DPDT switch, which you'll wire in an H-bridge configuration to reverse the motor when the lever is pressed. Then you'll mount a standoff for the comb to rest on so that once the bot is powered up, the comb can move back and forth in order to press the switch. After completing the switch assembly, you'll attach caster mounts to the plastic container lids to function as the bot's "feet." Then you'll attach the caster mounts to the end of each ruler section. Your final tasks will be to attach the battery holder to the circuit, clean up the wires, and insert the batteries to make the bot go.

Constructing Inchworm

Step 1. Cut the ruler into two 9-inch sections with the hacksaw.

Step 1

Step 2. On one of the 9-inch sections, make two cuts three-quarters of the way through the ruler at ½ inch from the end and 2⅛ inches from the same end.

Step 2

Step 3. Place the ruler in a bench vise so that the bottom of the cuts is level with the top of the vise. Hammer the section between the two cuts flat such that it's perpendicular to the ruler. This will be your motor mount.

Step 4. Place your servo motor into the slot you just cut, and use a pencil to mark where its mounting holes are.

Step 3

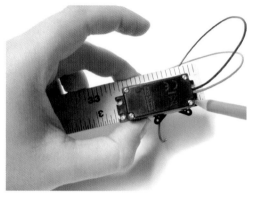

Step 4

Step 5. Drill through the marks on the ruler with a ⅛-inch drill bit.

Step 6. Drill a ¼-inch hole that is ½ inch from the edge of one of the cut ruler sections. Repeat this for the second section of ruler.

Step 5

Step 6

Step 7. Drill a ⅛-inch hole in each end of the servo horn. Detach the servo horn from your servo once you have drilled the holes.

Step 8. Center the servo horn on the section of ruler without the motor mount, roughly 1¼ inch in from the edge of the ruler that has not yet been drilled. Use it as a guide to both mark and drill four ⅛-inch holes through the ruler.

Step 7   Step 8

Step 9. Drill a ⅛-inch hole, centered upon the ruler section with the motor mount, that is 5 inches from the edge with the mount.

Drill a ³⁄₁₆-inch hole into the ruler section with the servo horn mount that is roughly 5 inches from the edge with the servo horn mount and close to the edge of the ruler.

Then, drill a second, larger ¼-inch hole that is 4 inches from the edge with the servo horn mount and centered on the ruler.

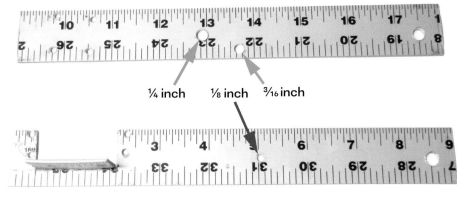

¼ inch   ⅛ inch   ³⁄₁₆ inch

Step 9

Step 10. Mount the motor to the ruler using nuts and bolts.

Step 11. Reattach the motor horn with its mounting screw.

Step 10   Step 11

Step 12. Use nuts and bolts to attach the other section of the ruler to the servo horn. The rulers should be able to move back and forth past each other as the motor spins.

Step 13. Use cutting pliers to remove 2 inches' worth of teeth from one side of your comb, stopping about ½ inch short of the edge. The few remaining teeth on the far edge will act as a safeguard to keep the comb on track.

When you're done removing teeth, sand that section of the comb smooth and then drill a ⅛-inch hole on the opposite edge.

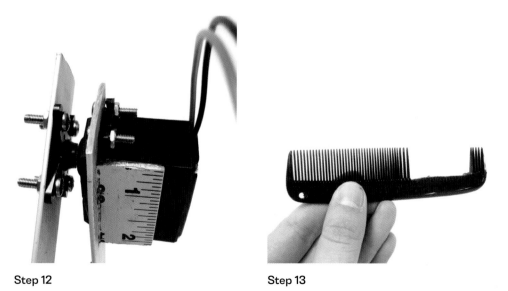

Step 12   Step 13

Step 14. Pass a bolt through the hole in the comb and then place two to four washers on it. The point of these washers is to push the comb toward the other section of ruler (once mounted).

Next, pass the screw through the middle hole in the section of the ruler with the motor. Use your bolt to fasten it securely in place.

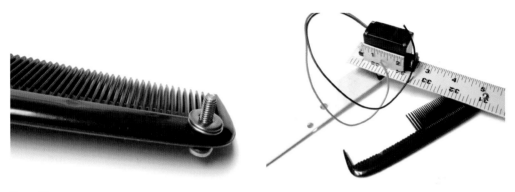

Step 14

Step 15. Position one of your switch's mounting nuts about ¼ inch from the bottom of the switch's threads.

Next, insert the DPDT switch into the ¼-inch hole that you drilled in the ruler in step 9.

Finally, lock the switch in place with its second mounting nut. The lever should now be about flush with the face of the ruler.

Step 15

Step 16. Wire together the opposite corners of the DPDT switch. Solder a long red battery wire to one of the center DPDT switch pins and a long black wire to the other. You'll eventually connect them to the battery holder.

Turn the switch so that only two pins are facing you (as opposed to three). Solder the black motor wire to the DPDT pin closest to you on the right. Solder the red motor wire to the other pin on the left.

Step 16

> ➡️ **NOTE** Refer to "H-Bridges" on page 30 in Chapter 3 for more information on how to change the direction a motor is spinning.

Step 17. Mount the standoff to the servo horn section of the ruler such that it is facing inward in the same direction as the lever switch. The comb will rest on top of the standoff.

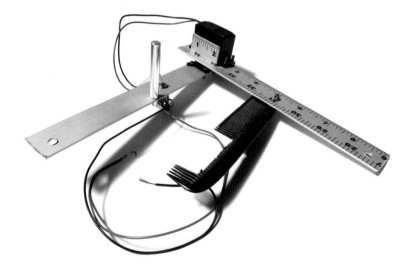

Step 17

Step 18. Now that you've assembled the body, you'll construct the inchworm's "feet." Take your two casters and remove the wheels. For many casters, this just means unscrewing a nut. However, if the wheels are riveted, you may need to drill through the rivet to remove them.

Step 18

Step 19. For each plastic container and caster mount pair, center the caster mount on top of the plastic container. Use the holes in the caster mount as guides for drilling ⅛-inch holes in the lid of the container.

Step 20. Zip-tie the caster frames in place to create pivots.

Step 19

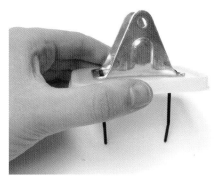

Step 20

Step 21. Drill a ⅛-inch hole in the corner of one of the container lids.

Step 22. Place the battery holder inside and pass the power wires through the hole.

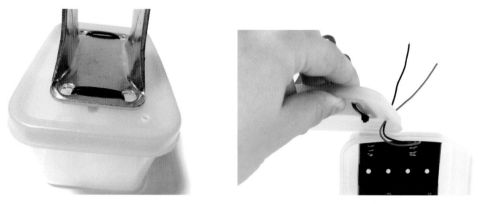

Step 21   Step 22

Step 23. Take your ballpoint pen and remove the ink cartridge, such that you're left with a hollow tube. With a cutting blade (such as a box cutter), cut the tube to create two 1-inch sections. Cut those two sections in half, creating four ½-inch spacers. Alternatively, you can buy four ½-inch spacers from the hardware store.

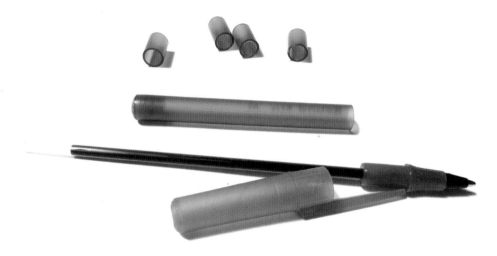

Step 23

Step 24. Reusing the caster's wheel mounting hardware, attach the rulers to the caster mounts using the cut pen spacers on each side of the rulers. If a ruler seems loose or tipsy, insert metal washers between the spacer and the ruler until it's no longer loose.

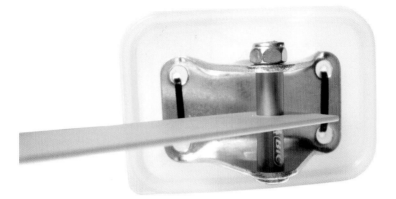

Step 24

Step 25. Solder the red wire from the switch to the red wire from the battery holder. Solder the black wire from the switch to the black wire from the battery holder.

Step 26. Cover the exposed connections in shrink tube to prevent the wires from shorting on the metal frame.

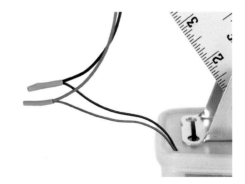

Step 25   Step 26

Step 27. Zip-tie all the loose wires together to prevent entanglement.

Step 27

Step 28. Insert some batteries and quickly close the plastic container lid to make the bot go.

> ➡️ **NOTE** If, when you power up the bot, the switch isn't making the motor move back and forth, remove the batteries, rotate the motor 180°, and try again.
>
> Be sure to remove the batteries to turn the bot off. See Appendix A for instructions on adding a power switch.

WALKER

My goal with Walker Bot was to build a four-legged walking bot that could be made in 10 minutes. This bot ultimately took 3 hours to make. That said, my goal wasn't to make one in 10 minutes myself, but to make one that *could* be made in 10 minutes. I'm pretty confident that, now that I know what I am doing, should I need to make a second one I could feasibly do it in 10 minutes. At the very least, you'll be hard-pressed to make a simpler walking bot than this one, so I consider this project a glowing success.

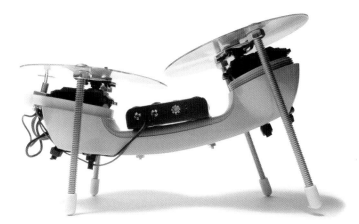

Tools and Supplies

- Two continuous-rotation servo motors with the controllers removed
- Four AA batteries
- A 4 × AA battery holder
- DPDT lever switch
- A "classic" telephone handset (search online for "vintage telephone handset")
- Two CDs (these should not be from anyone's music collection)
- Two ¼-20 × 6-inch bolts
- Two ¼-20 × 5-inch bolts
- Four ¼-20 nuts
- Four ¼-inch rubber bolt covers
- Two 4-40 × 1-inch nuts and bolts
- Roll of painter's tape
- An assortment of zip ties
- Cut template (see Appendix B)
- Drill
- Three drill bits: ¼, ⅛, and ³⁄₁₆ inch
- Scissors
- Cutting pliers
- Wire stripper

Walker Overview

To build Walker Bot, you'll use the same modified servo motors (Chapter 4) or the geared motor alternatives (Appendix A) used for the previous bots. Once you've modified the motors, the next step will be to take apart the telephone handset and place the servos where the microphone and speaker used to be. From there, you'll zip-tie the DPDT switch to one end of the headset. Next, you'll mount the battery holder to the telephone handset's handle, and you'll wire the switch in an H-bridge configuration to complete the circuit. Then, you'll trace and cut out or print the CD cutting templates, which you'll tape to the CDs (or DVDs). You'll use these templates as guides for drilling and cutting the appropriate holes and shapes into the CDs. Once this is completed, you'll zip-tie the CDs to the motors and insert bolts through the CDs to act as legs. Finally, you'll insert batteries and put Walker Bot down so it can walk around.

Constructing Walker

Step 1. Widen the second-from-last hole on each end of the motor horns using a ⅛-inch drill bit.

Step 2. Remove the covers from the telephone handset and then pull out the speaker, microphone, and jack. They should come right out.

Step 1

Step 3. Drill four ³⁄₁₆-inch holes in each end of the telephone handset, as pictured. Essentially, you should drill the holes so that they create a square on the backside of each opening.

Step 4. Starting on the side of the handset opposite where the jack was, pass the motor's wires through the body of the phone and out the hole created by removing

Step 2

the jack. Insert the first motor into the handset opening on the opposite side of the jack so that the horn faces inward.

Step 3

Step 4

Step 5. Pass the second motor's wires through the hole created by the jack and insert that motor into the end of the handset. Make certain that the horn for this motor also faces inward. Zip-tie them both in place using the holes you drilled earlier.

Step 6. Zip-tie the DPDT switch to the round mouthpiece opening, right above the hole created by removing the jack. There should be a small lip upon which the switch can sit. Make certain that the lever of the switch points upward (toward the gear on the motor).

Step 7. Using the mounting holes in the battery pack as guides, drill two ⅛-inch holes into the center of the handset such that they line up with the mounting holes of your AA battery holder.

Step 8. Bolt the battery holder onto the handset with your pair of 1-inch nuts and bolts.

Step 5

Step 6

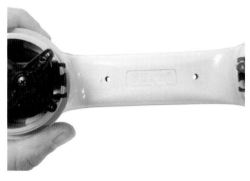

Step 7

Step 8

Step 9. Solder the red and black wires from the battery holder to each of the center terminals of the DPDT switch.

Solder two short wires to form an X between the outer terminals of the switch. Basically, the back left should be connected to the front right, and the front left to the back right. This causes power to be applied backward when the switch is flipped.

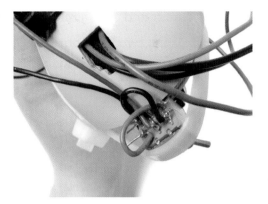

Step 9

Solder together the red wire from motor one with the black wire from motor two, and solder the black wire from motor one with the red wire from motor two (which motor is designated to be which is unimportant).

Finally, solder the red and black wire pairs to either set of outer terminals. For instance, solder one pair to the back-left terminal and the other pair to the back-right terminal.

> ➡ **NOTE** Refer to the "H-Bridges" section on page 30 in Chapter 3 for more information on how to change the direction a motor is spinning.

Step 10. To prepare the CDs (or DVDs) that will mount to the bot, trace the cutting templates and then cut out the two large circles.

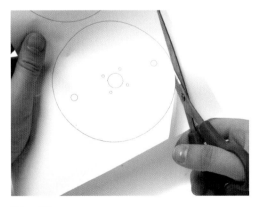

Step 10

Step 11. Center and tape a template on top of each CD.

Step 12. For the two large outer circles, drill ¼-inch holes. For the four smaller inner circles, drill ⅛-inch holes.

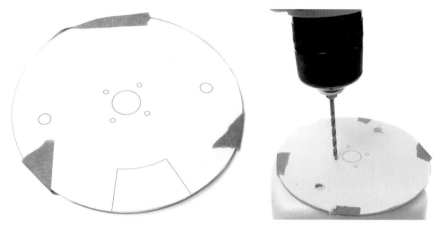

Step 11   Step 12

Step 13. Find the CD with the outer notch and cut it out carefully with scissors.

Step 13

Step 14. Zip-tie the CDs to the motors so that the two outer holes on each CD are perpendicular to the handset and the CD with the outer notch aligns with the lever from the DPDT toggle switch.

Step 14

Step 15. Pass the shorter 5-inch bolts through the notched CD. Pass the longer 6-inch bolts upward through the other CD. Fasten all of them in place with nuts.

Step 16. Cover all of the bolts with rubber bolt covers to give them a bit more traction.

Step 15   Step 16

Step 17. Insert the batteries and then let the bot go.

> **NOTE** If, when you power up the bot, the switch doesn't make the motor move back and forth, remove the batteries, rotate the switch 180°, and try again.

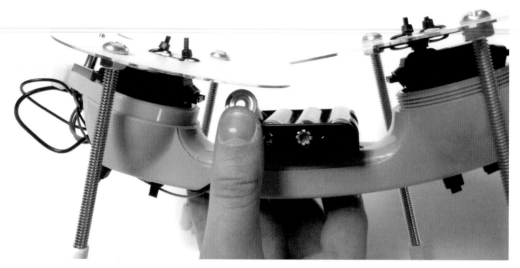

Step 17

> ➡ **NOTE** Be sure to remove the batteries to turn the bot off. See Appendix A for instructions on adding a power switch.

13

SAIL

When Sail Bot encounters headwinds, it turns to avoid them. Unlike the previous bots with DPDT switches that change direction only when they press their own levers, Sail Bot momentarily changes direction only when wind activates its lever. In other words, when there is a gust of wind, the bot turns to avoid it; otherwise, Sail Bot goes about its business. Although it may seem simple, this behavior is actually fairly complex, considering that the circuit, in a sense, is just a collection of switches.

Tools and Supplies

- Two continuous-rotation servo motors with the controllers removed
- A 4 × 9½ × 2-inch plastic utensil holder
- A 4 × AA battery holder
- Four AA batteries
- A 6 V DPDT relay
- Relay socket
- Two 3-inch casters
- A 1½-inch swivel caster
- One 8 × 8-inch corrugated plastic sheet
- Drill
- A ⅛-inch drill bit
- A ¾-inch spade bit
- Wire cutter
- Wire stripper
- Roll of stranded wire
- Screwdriver
- Marker
- Pliers
- Ruler
- Assorted zip ties

Sail Overview

To build Sail Bot, you first need to modify two continuous-rotation servos for direct drive by removing their controller boards (Chapter 4) or use two geared motor alternatives, as outlined in Appendix A. Next, you'll mount the servos to the inside of the utensil holder. From there, you'll attach the swivel caster to the bottom of the utensil holder. You'll wire up the circuit to the relay socket (or directly to the relay) and install it in the utensil holder. Then you'll construct the sail mechanism and firmly attach it to the relay. Finally, you'll attach the wheels to the servos and insert batteries to make the bot go.

Constructing Sail

Step 1. Remove the wheels from the 3-inch caster frames by undoing the nuts and bolts holding them onto the frames.

Step 1

Step 2. Widen the second-from-last hole in each end of the servo horns using a ⅛-inch drill bit.

Step 3. Undo the mounting screws to remove the servo horns from the servos. Set the screws aside for later.

Step 2   Step 3

Step 4. Center a servo horn on each wheel and use a thin screwdriver to press marks into the frame of each wheel to use as drill guides.

Step 5. Use the indents you just made as guides to drill ⅛-inch holes straight down through the wheels.

Step 4   Step 5

Step 6. Zip-tie the servo horns to the wheels and trim away the remaining tails.

Step 7. Insert the DPDT relay into the socket simply by pressing it down firmly.

Step 6

Step 8. On the outside of the utensil holder, position a servo motor on one of the bottom corners of the long edge, with the servo shaft facing inward. Make marks to represent each of the servo's mounting holes and the servo shaft. Mirror this on the opposite side of the utensil holder.

Step 9. Drill the outer marks for the servo mounting holes with a ⅛-inch drill bit and then drill the center servo shaft marks with a ¾-inch spade bit.

Step 7

Step 8

Step 9

Step 10. Place the servos on the inside of the utensil holder, zip-tie them firmly into place, and then trim the remaining zip-tie tails.

Step 11. Place the 1½-inch caster on the bottom of the utensil holder on the end opposite from the servo motors. Make marks in each of the caster's mounting holes.

Step 10   Step 11

Step 12. Drill each mark with a ⅛-inch drill bit.

Step 13. Zip-tie the 1½-inch caster to the underside of the utensil holder.

Step 12   Step 13

Step 14. Solder a 6-inch black wire to the common connection of the switch and a 6-inch red wire to the normally open (NO) connection.

Step 15. Next, wire the circuit using the following diagram as a reference. You can learn more about how this circuit works in Appendix A on page 160.

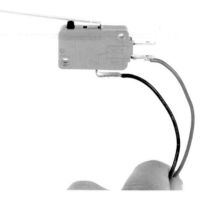

Step 14

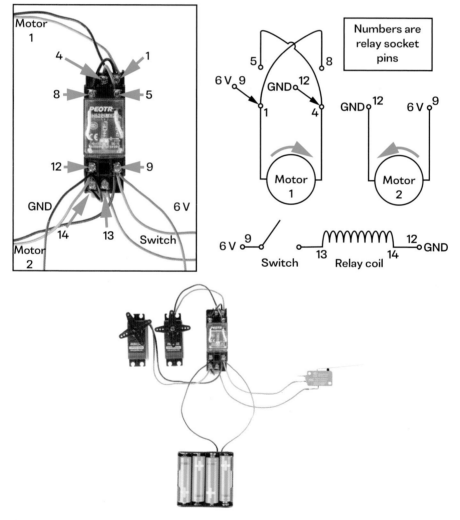

Step 15

Step 16. Insert batteries briefly to test the circuit.

If your motors are spinning backward from how you expected, reverse the connection of the motor wires to the relay.

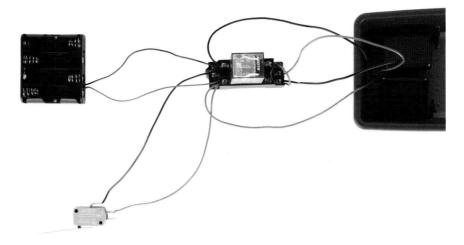

Step 16

Step 17. Place the DPDT relay socket in the bottom of the utensil holder near the servos.

Make two marks on each side of the DPDT relay socket, creating four marks in all, that you'll use to zip-tie the socket in place.

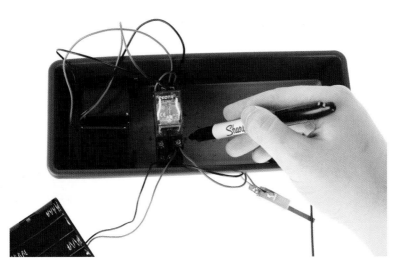

Step 17

Step 18. Drill each of the four marks for mounting the DPDT relay with a ⅛-inch drill bit.

Step 19. Secure the relay socket in place using zip ties and the mounting holes.

Step 18

Step 19

Step 20. The corrugated sheet will be used as a sail. Slide the snap-action switch's lever into one of the center openings in the corrugated sheet until it is firmly in place.

Step 20

Step 21. Zip-tie the switch to the side of the relay such that the sail is facing toward the front of the bot (the side with the small caster).

If the sail is too heavy for the switch and keeps it compressed, you can either cut the sail smaller or lean the switch forward a little bit.

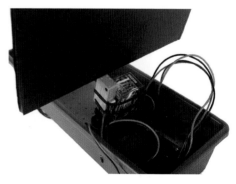

Step 21

Step 22. Attach the 3-inch wheels to the servos using the servo horns' mounting screws.

Step 22

Step 23. Insert the batteries into the battery holder and watch the bot set sail.

Step 23

When wind blows the sail, one wheel should spin in the opposite direction and cause the bot to rotate away from the wind. Once the bot has turned away from the wind, the bot will resume driving forward.

> **NOTE** Be sure to remove the batteries to turn the bot off. See Appendix A for instructions on adding a power switch.

14

FLIP FLOP

F lip Flop Bot is a prime example of a *state machine*, as it follows a specific routine and has different modes of operation. For instance, if the first set of switches is activated, the bot is in its first mode and travels in a forward direction. If the other set of switches is activated, the bot is in its second mode and travels in a backward direction. Essentially, this bot drives forward until it hits something, and then it reverses and goes the other way until it hits something else. If you put the bot in a door frame, it travels back and forth endlessly (or until the batteries run out).

If you want to create something a little more dynamic, swap out the round wheels for wheels of a different shape (oval perhaps). Then Flip Flop Bot will no longer travel back and forth in a straight line continuously.

The beauty of this bot is that it can change its state and then stay in that new state until it receives new input.

Tools and Supplies

- Two continuous-rotation servo motors with the controllers removed
- A 4 × AA battery holder
- Four AA batteries
- Two 3-inch casters
- Two 3-inch round reflectors
- A 6 V 3PDT relay
- A 3PDT relay socket
- An 8 × 5 × 1-inch tray (or similar)
- Four snap-action lever switches
- Two ¼-20 leveling mounts
- A ⅜-inch diameter shrink tube
- Four 8-inch zip ties
- Assorted zip ties
- Saw
- Drill
- A ⅛-inch drill bit
- A ¼-inch drill bit
- Wire stripper
- Diagonal cutting pliers
- Screwdriver
- Ruler
- Marker

Flip Flop Overview

To make this bot, first modify two continuous-rotation servos for direct drive by removing their controller boards (Chapter 4) or use two geared motor alternatives, as outlined in Appendix A. You'll drill the servo horns and attach them to the caster wheels. From there, you'll mark and modify the tray to attach it to the servo motors. You'll wire up each pair of switches, attaching them to the reflectors and attaching the reflectors to the tray. Then, you'll wire up the whole circuit using a 3PDT relay. This is similar to a DPDT relay (or switch) but has an additional set of SPDT pins built in. You can learn more about this relay in Appendix A on page 161. Once that is wired, you'll secure the relay and reattach the wheels. To complete the bot, you'll add zip-tie antennae to the switches, and you'll be ready to power up the bot.

Constructing Flip Flop

Step 1. Remove the center bolts to separate the wheels from the caster frames.

Step 2. Widen the second-from-the-last hole in each end of the servo horn using a ⅛-inch drill bit. Repeat for the other servo horn.

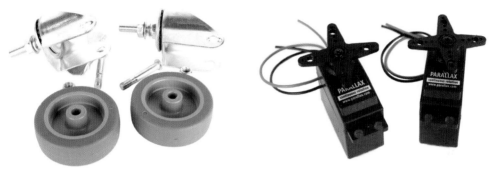

Step 1   Step 2

Step 3. Undo the mounting screws to remove the servo horns from the servos.

Step 4. Center a servo horn on each wheel and use a thin screwdriver to press marks into the frame of each wheel to use as drill guides.

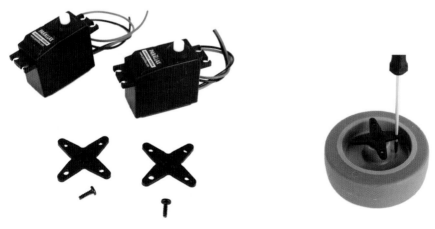

Step 3   Step 4

Step 5. Use the indents you just made as guides to drill ⅛-inch holes straight down through the wheels.

Step 6. Zip-tie the servo horns to the wheels and trim away the remaining tails.

Step 5

Step 6

Step 7. Make a mark centered on each of the long edges of the tray.

Step 8. Line up the servo shaft with the center marks and then trace two cut marks onto each long edge of the tray to outline the body of the servo.

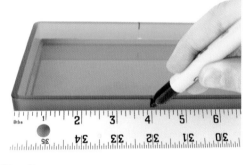

Step 7

Step 8

Step 9. With the lines you drew in step 8 as a guide, use a saw to cut out a hole large enough to insert the motor into it on each long side of the tray. The motors should be resting along the bottom of the tray.

Step 10. Make marks to indicate the servo mounting holes along the edge of the tray. If only the bottommost holes line up with the edge of the tray, it's okay.

Step 9   Step 10

Step 11. Drill through the marks on the sides of the tray using a ⅛-inch drill bit.

Step 12. Zip-tie the motors to the edges of the tray.

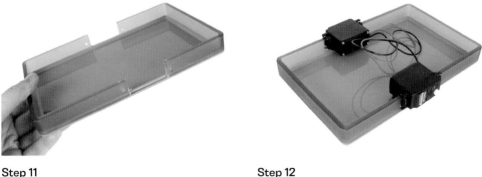

Step 11   Step 12

Step 13. Stack two switches along the edge of each round reflector. Make marks on each reflector on both sides of the switch to serve as drill guides for a zip tie.

Step 14. Make another mark roughly in the center of each reflector.

Step 13

Step 14

Step 15. Drill all the marks on the reflectors with a ⅛-inch drill bit.

Step 16. Peel the adhesive back from each reflector and stick a switch along the edge between the ⅛-inch holes.

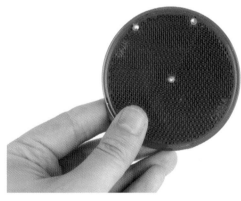

Step 15

Step 16

Step 17. Stack another switch on top of the one on the adhesive reflector and zip-tie it in place. Repeat this process with the remaining reflector and lever switches.

Step 18. One pair of switches should have their normally closed (NC) connections wired *in series*. This means you need to wire the common pins together, attach a long red wire to the NC pin on one switch, and attach a long black wire to the NC pin on the other switch.

Step 17

The other pair of switches should have their NO (normally open) connections wired *in parallel*. This means you need to wire the common pins together and then wire the NO pins together. Finally, attach a long red wire to the NO connections and a long black wire to the common connections.

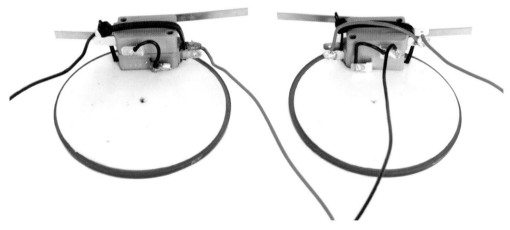

Step 18

Step 19. Stick one of the reflectors to the bottom of the tray such that the switch is right up against one of the short edges of the tray.

Step 20. Attach the remaining adhesive reflector to the bottom of the tray along the other short edge.

Step 19   Step 20

Step 21. Drill through both the center of the reflector and the tray using a ¼-inch drill bit.

Step 21

Step 22. Attach the leveling mounts directly below the reflectors and lock them in place with their mounting nuts.

Step 22

Step 23. Place the relay socket on top of the tray and make two marks along both edges to indicate where its mounting holes will be.

Step 24. Drill each of the four markings with a ⅛-inch drill bit.

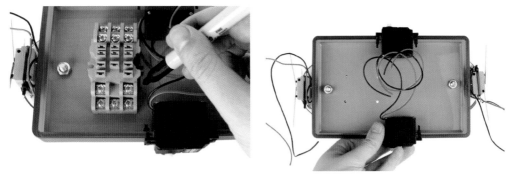

Step 23   Step 24

Step 25. Build the circuit using the relay socket as outlined in the following wiring diagram. Go slow and make sure that all the correct connections to the relay socket terminals are made. You can learn more about how this circuit works in Appendix A on page 161. When you are done building the circuit, the motors, switches, and battery holder should all be wired to the relay socket, as shown.

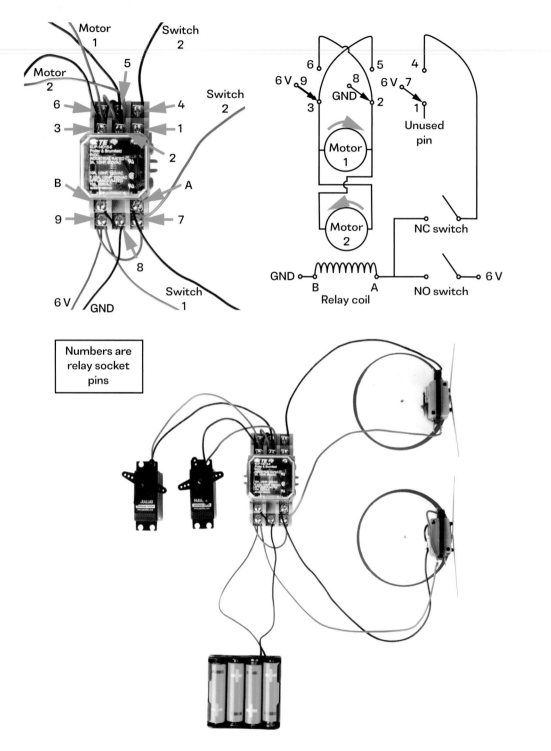

Motor 1

Switch 2

Motor 2

5

6

4

Switch 2

3

1

2

B

A

9

7

8

6 V

GND

Switch 1

6

5

4

6 V 9

8

6 V 7

GND

3

2

1

Unused pin

Motor 1

Motor 2

NC switch

GND

B   A
Relay coil

NO switch

6 V

Numbers are relay socket pins

Step 25

Step 26. Insert the 3PDT relay into the relay socket.

Step 27. Attach the wheels to the servo hubs using the servo horns' mounting screws.

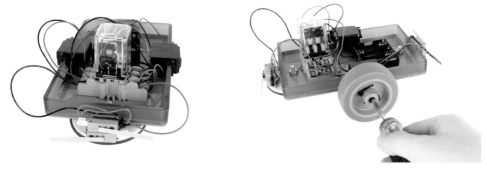

Step 26   Step 27

Step 28. Zip-tie the relay socket firmly to the bottom of the tray. While you are at it, you can optionally clean up the wires using zip ties as well.

Step 29. Slide the shrink tube all the way onto the 8-inch zip ties. Then slide the shrink tube and zip-tie assemblies onto each lever of the snap-action switches to create antennae. Once these are positioned, use a heat gun to shrink the tubing. You can also use tape if you don't have shrink tube.

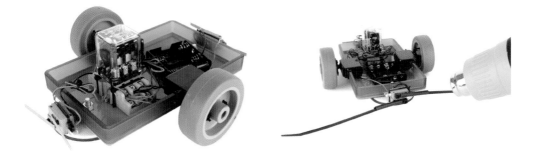

Step 28   Step 29

Step 30. Insert the batteries into the battery holder and let the bot go.

When the bot collides with an object, the switches should compress, and the bot should reverse. If it doesn't behave as expected, check your wiring against the diagram. See Appendix A for a more detailed description of this circuit.

Step 30

> **NOTE** Be sure to remove the batteries to turn the bot off. See Appendix A for instructions on adding a power switch.

REFERENCE
MATERIALS

Some of the techniques and concepts in this book are more advanced, so some readers may want alternatives or additional background information. Over the next few pages, you will find alternative methods to challenging techniques, an in-depth explanation of relay circuits, instructions for adding a power switch to any bot, an electronics shopping list, and a list of reference materials. For even more information, visit *http://www.randysarafan.com/*.

Alternatives to Soldering

If soldering is not your thing, you can make electrical connections and circuits using other methods. The following is a brief overview of some techniques.

ALLIGATOR CLIPS

Alligator clip jumper cables (as seen in Chapter 2 on page 19) essentially are wires with alligator clips on both ends. They provide a quick and easy way to connect nearly anything together, as long as the electrical contact can fit in the clip's mouth. Alligator clips are great for attaching wires, switches, and motor terminals together temporarily. Keep in mind that while these connections are convenient for prototyping, they aren't the most durable of connections.

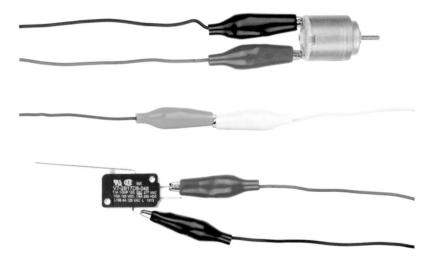

CRIMP CONNECTORS

Crimp connectors provide another easy way to join wires together without soldering. By crimping or clamping a connector onto the end of each wire, you can join two wires together. Sometimes crimp connectors simply slide together, and sometimes you need additional hardware, like a nut and bolt, to keep them together. The downsides to crimp connectors are that they're a little bulky and the electrical connections are exposed and need to be insulated.

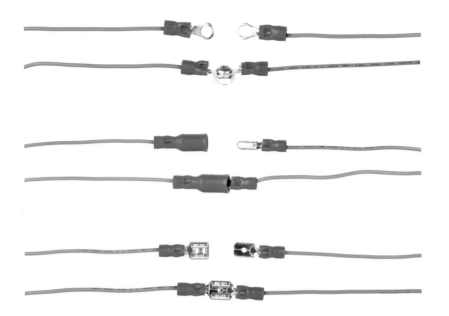

To crimp the connector onto the wire, strip about ½ inch of insulation off the end of the wire and slide the wire into the barrel of the connector. Then, compress the barrel to grab onto the wire. Place the connector on a sturdy, flat surface and bash the connector's barrel with a hammer until it is flat.

Alternatively, many wire strippers have a crimping tool on the inner handle. If your wire stripper has this feature, line up the groove in the crimping tool that matches the size of your wire and then squeeze down firmly.

LEVERS, SPRINGS, AND SCREWS

Another quick and dirty way to connect wires together involves using a mechanical lever, spring connector, or screw terminal. They all work in a similar way. Start by lifting the lever, pressing down on the spring-loaded button, or unthreading the screw to open the connector. Next, insert the wire, and then press the lever, release the spring, or tighten the screw to hold the wire in place and make an electrical connection. This method is one of the fastest and easiest ways to connect wires together; however, these connectors are bulky, and with enough force, you can potentially pull the wires loose.

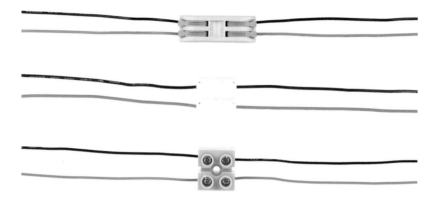

BARREL AND SOCKET CONNECTORS

Last but not least, you can use barrel and socket connectors with screw terminals to make power connections. If you want to connect batteries to one or more parallel motors, simply attach one connector to a battery pack and the other to a motor by inserting the wires into the connector's screw terminals. Finally, insert the barrel plug into the barrel socket, and you're in business.

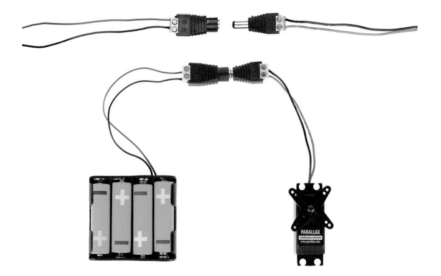

Alternatives to Servo Motors

Controllerless servo motors are the best solution for building the bots in this book, but some other approaches could provide similar results.

All of these alternative methods basically consist of three elements: a geared motor, a motor mounting bracket, and some sort of wheel or disc that attaches to the motor shaft.

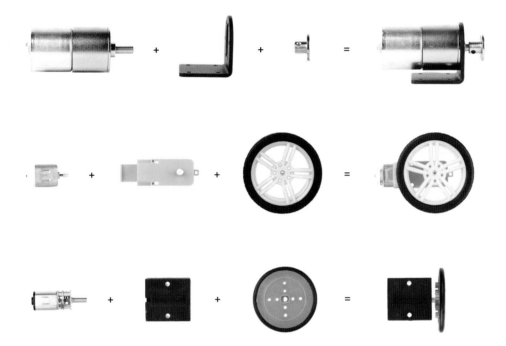

This list is by no means comprehensive, so feel free to experiment and find other solutions. If you stick to this formula, you can't go wrong.

> **NOTE** Keep in mind that if you use an alternative motor to the controllerless servo motor, some measurements might change.

Relay Circuits

When using a relay, I recommend choosing a relay socket. Relay sockets have screw terminals that make it easy to connect and disconnect wires, although you can always attach wires directly to the relay pins.

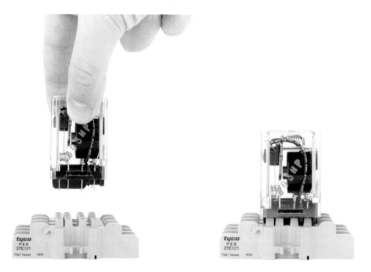

To insert a wire, simply loosen the screw, stick the uninsulated part of the wire under the screw (or screw plate), and then tighten it.

You can also easily add multiple wires to a single terminal.

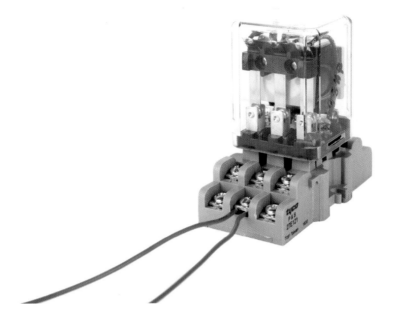

DPDT RELAY CIRCUITS

A DPDT relay works the same as a DPDT switch. In the preceding example, the terminals are wired in an H-bridge configuration (see page 30 in Chapter 3). The lever switch makes or breaks the power connection to the electromagnetic coil. If the coil is powered, the motor drives backward. If the coil is unpowered, the motor drives forward.

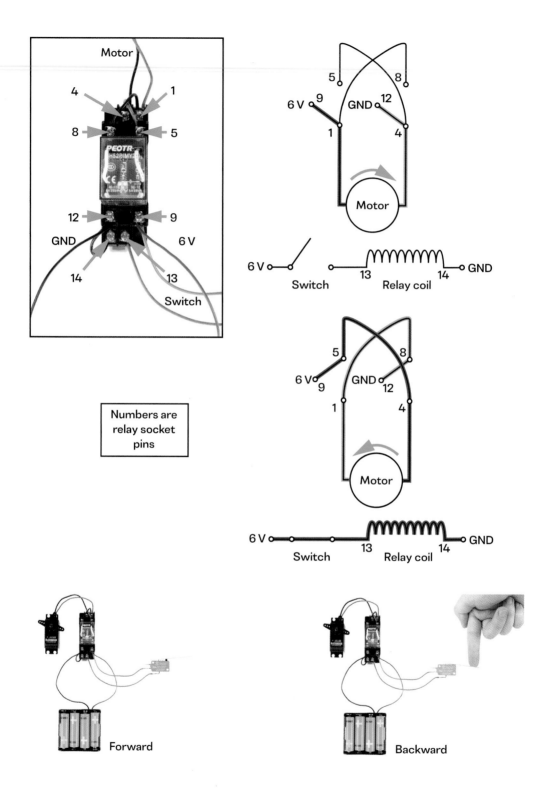

Motor

4   1
8   5
PEOTR
H52BIMY
12   9
GND   6 V
14   13
Switch

5   8
6 V 9   GND 12
1   4

Motor

6 V o──────o   o─────^^^^^^^─────o GND
      Switch   13   Relay coil   14

5   8
6 V 9   GND 12
1   4

Motor

6 V o────o────o───^^^^^^^───o GND
      Switch   13   Relay coil   14

Numbers are
relay socket
pins

Forward

Backward

3PDT RELAY CIRCUITS

You also can wire a 3PDT relay in an H-bridge configuration like a DPDT relay, but a 3PDT relay will have an unused set of SPDT relay terminal connections left over at the end. You can use that leftover set of terminals to control something else when the relay is activated.

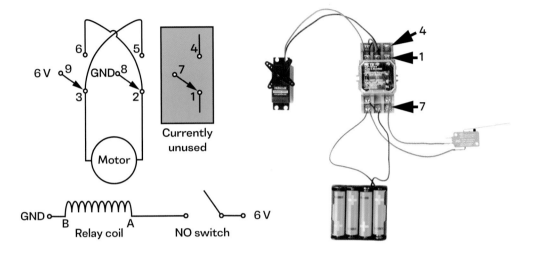

You can make a circuit that changes the motor direction (and stays changed) depending on which switch is pressed. All you need is this extra set of terminals and an additional SPDT lever switch. Flip Flop Bot from Chapter 14 uses this circuit.

This circuit consists of two switches that each power the coil using separate electrical paths. One path passes through the first switch wired to be normally open (NO). To do this, connect a wire to its NO connection as well as to its common C connection and the relay coil. The second path passes through two of the relay terminals not being used for the H-bridge. To do this, wire a switch to be normally closed (NC) by connecting a wire to its NC connection as well as to its common C connection and the relay coil.

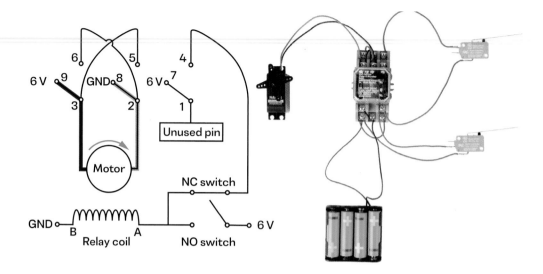

When the first normally open (NO) switch is pressed, the circuit completes. Power can now flow through the coil, and it becomes energized. This toggles the relay that reverses the motor direction using the H-bridge wiring. It also completes the second switch circuit that powers the coil.

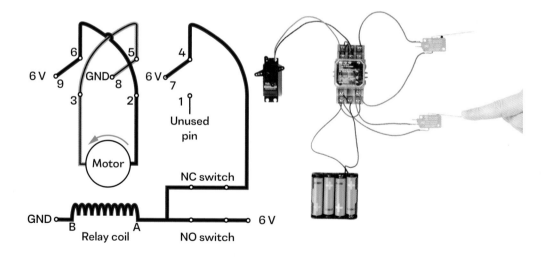

When the normally open (NO) switch is released, power stops flowing through it to the coil. However, power continues to flow through the other normally closed (NC) switch to the coil. As long as this switch remains closed, the coil will remain powered and the motor will continue spinning in reverse. If you want the motor to spin forward again, the only way is to break the electrical connection to the circuit by pressing the normally closed (NC) switch.

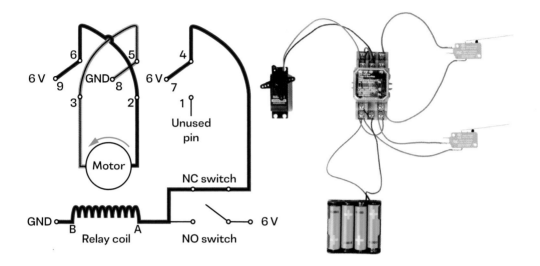

When the normally closed (NC) switch is pressed, the switch opens and breaks the circuit connection to the relay coil, which toggles the relay terminals, causing the motor to spin forward once again. This also breaks the power connection inside the relay to the normally closed (NC) switch, preventing it from powering the coil. From here, the process can start over again.

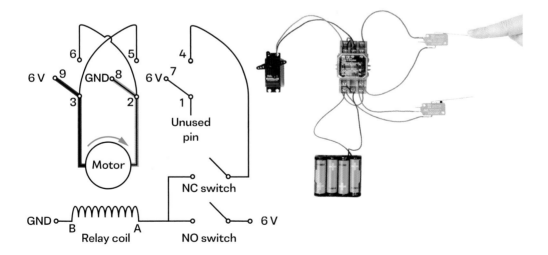

Adding a Power Switch

The bots in this book do not have power switches. However, adding a power switch to any bot is simple. Just gather an SPST toggle switch and follow these easy steps:

Step 1. Cut in half the red power wire connected to the battery pack.

Step 2. Solder each of the ends of wire to a terminal on an SPST switch.

Step 3. Drill a ¼-inch hole in the bot's enclosure in a spot where there is room to mount the switch.

Step 4. Insert the switch through the hole in the enclosure and fasten it in place with its mounting hardware.

Enjoy your new power switch!

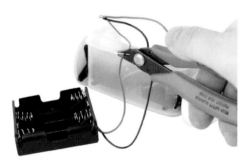

Step 1

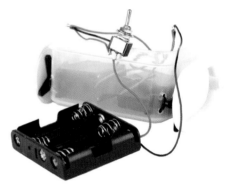

Step 2

Step 3

Step 4

Basic Electronics Shopping List

The following table lists the bare minimum parts needed to complete any project in this book, broken down according to chapter, including different electronics suppliers and part numbers.

> **NOTE** Some of these parts may become discontinued or the part numbers may change (particularly at Amazon). On these sites, you can simply search for the name of the part itself.

QUANTITY	PART	AMAZON	DIGIKEY	MOUSER	CHAPTER(S)	NOTES
2	Continuous servos	B01HSX1IDE	900-00008-ND	619-900-00008	5, 6, 7, 8, 9, 10, 11, 12, 13, 14	Used in all projects
1	4 × AA battery pack	B07F43VWRQ	36-2478-ND	534-2478	5, 6, 8, 11, 12, 13, 14	
1	3 × AA battery pack	B008HJ02F4	36-2480-ND	546-BH3AAW	7, 9, 10	
1	DPDT switch	B07QGBW6XZ	EG2398-ND	612-100-F1111	10, 11, 12	
1	SPST switch	B07QGDDTWJ	360-2827-ND	633-M201101	Appendix A	Optional power switch for all projects
2	Magnet reed SPDT switch	B0010F0086	—	507-AMS-505-392W	9	
1	Tilt switch	B07S9KQYNV	CKN10375-ND	611-RB-231X2	8	
4	Lever switch	B07YQPSK3B	480-5932-ND	785-V15T16-EZ100A03	13, 14	
1	22 AWG red stranded core wire	B07JNRJW37	422010RD005-ND	602-422010-100-03	5, 6, 7, 8, 9, 10, 11, 12, 13, 14	Used in all projects
1	22 AWG black stranded core wire	B07JNRJW37	422010BK005-ND	602-422010-100-02	5, 6, 7, 8, 9, 10, 11, 12, 13, 14	Used in all projects
1	3PDT relay – 6 V coil	B084KYCXQ8	KUP-14D15-6	655-KUP-14D15-6	14	
1	3PDT relay socket	B07J66JGZ3	PB165-ND	655-27E121	14	
1	DPDT relay – 6 V coil	B07SYHCPQX	PB2272-ND	655-KUP-11A15-6	13	
1	DPDT relay socket	B07SYHCPQX	PB166-ND	655-27E893	13	

Additional Resources

instructables.com You can find thousands of user-submitted robotics and electronics projects on this website. It also provides resources for learning other skills, such as fabrication and 3D printing.

Electronics for Kids by Øyvind Nydal Dahl A great book for diving deeper into electronic components and circuitry, with a series of fun hands-on projects.

Getting Started with Arduino by Massimo Banzi and Michael Shiloh A crash course on the basics of the Arduino microcontroller system from the inventor of the Arduino and another maker legend.

Arduino Project Handbook by Mark Geddes Another Arduino crash course with 25 hands-on projects that teach a wide array of Arduino skills (such as arrays).

Physical Computing by Dan O'Sullivan and Tom Igoe An advanced introduction to all things related to electronics. It reads more like a textbook than an activity book, but it's a good place to start to learn to build more advanced circuits.

Making Things Move by Dustyn Roberts Like *Physical Computing*, this book is more textbook than activity book, but it's approachable enough to give you a crash course on mechatronics.

Make: magazine A magazine at the forefront of the maker movement. It often has great articles about robots in addition to many other interesting topics.

HackSpace magazine Another great resource for staying current on DIY robotics and electronics.

hackerspaces.org On this website, you can find local hackerspaces and meet other people interested in robotics.

makerfaire.com Maker Faires are local and regional yearly events where makers come together and share their projects.

CUTTING AND
DRILLING TEMPLATES

I n this appendix, I've included the templates needed to make Barreller, Daze, and Walker. The easiest way to use these templates is by placing a regular sheet of white printer paper over the page and tracing the outlines with a pencil. Once you have traced the template onto the sheet of paper, you can cut it out and tape it to the part you are trying to cut or drill. For downloadable and printable versions of these templates, you can visit *http://www.randysarafan.com/* or *https://nostarch.com/homemaderobots/*.

Daze

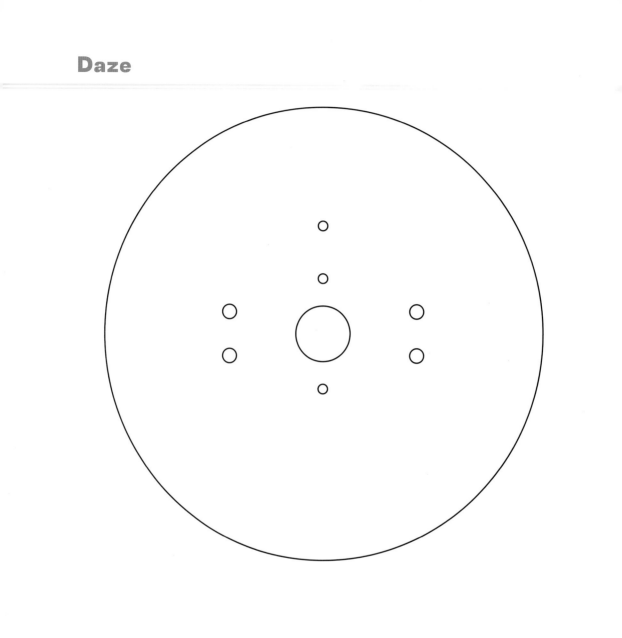

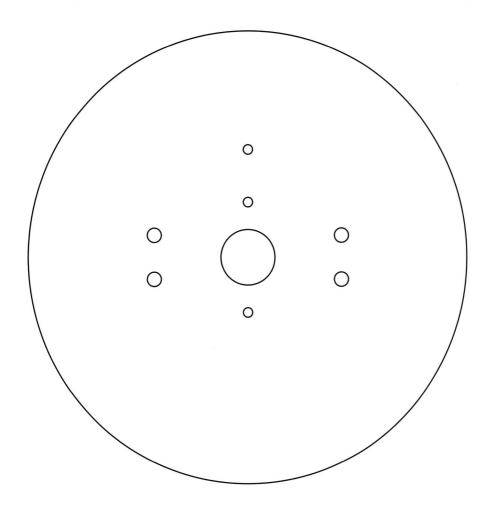

Barreller

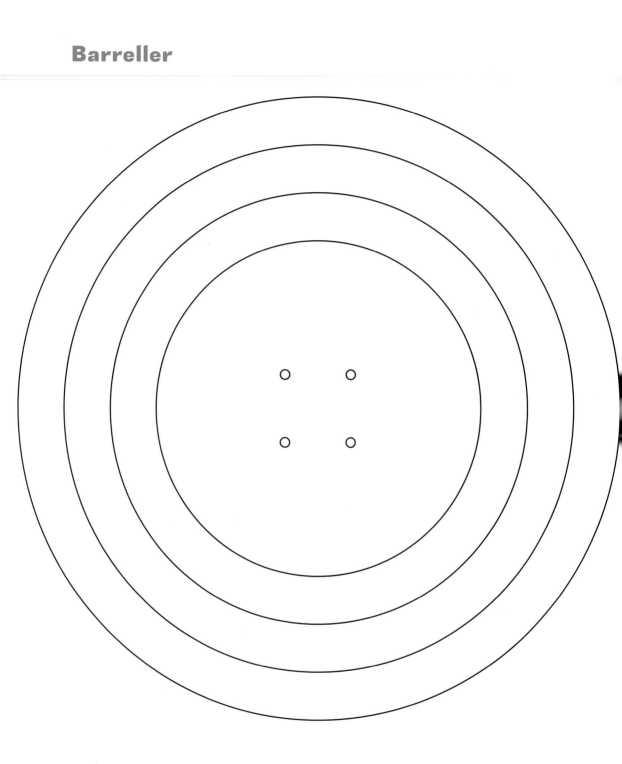

Walker

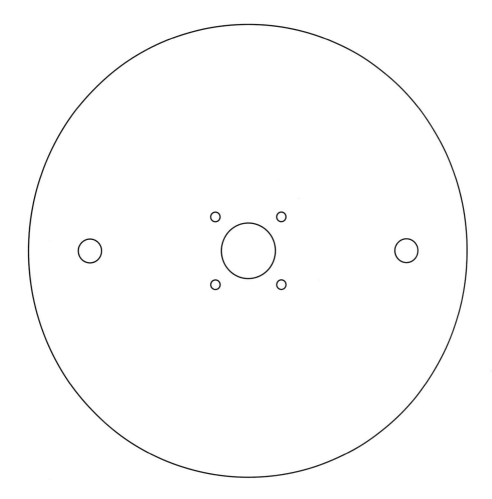

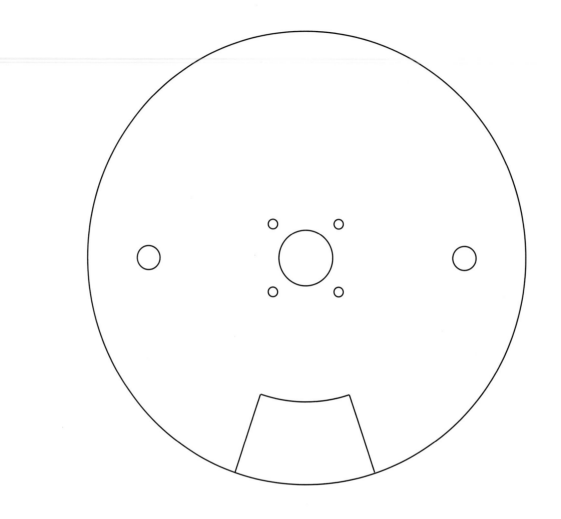

INDEX

Italicized page numbers indicate definitions of terms.